What Readers Are Saying About
The Treasure Principle

"Finally, a book that is able to encourage joyful, sacrificial grace giving without browbeating people with a guilt trip! Finally, a book that takes a scripturally sound approach to this important area of Christian doctrine and practice!"
—V. V.

"This book is fantastic. It is concise, motivational, and profound. This would be a great book to study with a small group."
—A. H.

"Other than the Bible itself, few books have changed my actions as quickly as this outstanding little book. I read it aloud to my husband, and together we made decisions about the money and possessions God has entrusted to our care. These choices have brought us great joy."
—F. E.

"Seldom do you find a book that distinguishes itself as head and shoulders above the rest, but this one does. It's one of the top books I've ever read."
—B. H., pastor

"*The Treasure Principle* has opened my eyes. A light has come on! I'm excited about stewardship."

—J. C.

"I have never had my perspectives so challenged. One hundred percent must-read."

—N. T.

"I'm just starting a sermon series on stewardship at my church, and *The Treasure Principle* is a piece of gold. I have rarely seen so much wisdom articulated with such simplicity, brevity, and conviction."

—M. B., pastor

"I loved this book. When you read the truth of God, it affects your soul. Though the concepts are simple, the life change is monumental. There is no prosperity gospel here, just truth."

—B. T.

THE TREASURE
PRINCIPLE

REVISED AND UPDATED EDITION

THE TREASURE PRINCIPLE

Unlocking the Secret of Joyful Giving

NEARLY 2 MILLION COPIES SOLD

RANDY ALCORN

MULTNOMAH

The Treasure Principle

All Scripture quotations, unless otherwise indicated, are taken from the Holy Bible, New International Version®, NIV®. Copyright © 1973, 1978, 1984 by Biblica Inc.® Used by permission. All rights reserved worldwide. Scripture quotations marked (ESV) are taken from the ESV® Bible (the Holy Bible, English Standard Version®), copyright © 2001 by Crossway, a publishing ministry of Good News Publishers. Used by permission. All rights reserved. Scripture quotations marked (GNT) are taken from the Good News Translation in Today's English Version—Second Edition. Copyright © 1992 by American Bible Society. Used by permission. Scripture quotations marked (NASB) are taken from the New American Standard Bible®. © Copyright © 1960, 1962, 1963, 1968, 1971, 1972, 1973, 1975, 1977, 1995 by the Lockman Foundation. Used by permission. (www.Lockman.org). Scripture quotations marked (NKJV) are taken from the New King James Version®. Copyright © 1982 by Thomas Nelson Inc. Used by permission. All rights reserved. Scripture quotations marked (NLT) are taken from the Holy Bible, New Living Translation, copyright © 1996, 2004, 2007, 2013, 2015 by Tyndale House Foundation. Used by permission of Tyndale House Publishers Inc., Carol Stream, Illinois 60188. All rights reserved.

Italics in Scripture quotations reflect the author's added emphasis.

Special Markets ISBN 978-0-525-61503-3

Copyright © 2001, 2017 by Eternal Perspective Ministries

Cover design by Kirk DouPonce, DogEaredDesign.com
Cover image by Dog Eared Design, LLC

Published in the United States by Multnomah, an imprint of the Crown Publishing Group, a division of Penguin Random House LLC, New York.

MULTNOMAH® and its mountain colophon are registered trademarks of Penguin Random House LLC.

Library of Congress Cataloging-in-Publication Data
Names: Alcorn, Randy C., author.
Title: The treasure principle : unlocking the secret of joyful giving / Randy Alcorn.
Description: Revised and Updated Edition. | Colorado Springs, Colorado : Multnomah, 2017. | Includes bibliographical references.
Identifiers: LCCN 2017008109| ISBN 9780735290327 (hardcover) | ISBN 9781588601223 (electronic)
Subjects: LCSH: Wealth—Religious aspects—Christianity. | Christian giving.
Classification: LCC BR115.W4 A44 2017 | DDC 248/.6—dc23 LC record available at https://lccn.loc.gov/2017008109

Printed in the United States of America
2017 Special Markets Edition

10 9 8 7 6 5 4 3

SPECIAL SALES
Most Multnomah books are available at special quantity discounts when purchased in bulk by corporations, organizations, and special-interest groups. Custom imprinting or excerpting can also be done to fit special needs. For information, please e-mail specialmarketscms@penguin randomhouse.com or call 1-800-603-7051.

*Thanks, Jim Lund, for your
servant's heart and your valued role
as the original editor on this book.
Thanks also to Laura Barker, Doreen
Button, Kathy Norquist, and Stephanie
Anderson for their editorial work on this
expanded and updated version.*

Contents

Preface to the Revised
and Updated 2017 Edition

When I was writing *The Treasure Principle* in 2000, someone on the publisher's marketing team said, "So we're going to ask people to spend money to buy your book so you can persuade them to give away lots of money?"

Well, there's more to it than that, but in a way the answer was *yes*. It's safe to say that seventeen years ago, when people were brainstorming book ideas with strong reader appeal, nobody—including me—was thinking, "I know—let's do a book about giving. It'll sell a million copies!"

Yet as I write this, *The Treasure Principle* has sold nearly two million copies. It has been distributed in thousands of churches and by hundreds of ministries. Businessmen and financial advisors routinely give it to their clients. The book has been translated into twenty-nine languages, including Chinese, Bengali, Croatian, Czech, Danish, Dutch, Greek, Indonesian, Korean, Japanese, Latvian, Russian, Serbian, Slovenian, Polish, Portuguese, Vietnamese, and Arabic.

God has used *The Treasure Principle,* as well as my larger work on stewardship, *Money, Possessions, and Eternity*[1], to play a strategic role in the Generous Giving movement (www .generousgiving.org) that has touched countless followers of

Christ and furthered missions and relief and development work worldwide.

I've received hundreds of letters and e-mails detailing radical choices, enduring life changes, and greatly multiplied joy as a result of embracing the truths in this book. One reader wrote, "I picked up *The Treasure Principle* and started reading aloud, and the Holy Spirit worked with lightning speed. I had perfect clarity of mission. It wasn't about me anymore."

A mother e-mailed, "My eleven-year-old son gets five dollars per week. We taught him that fifty cents was his tithe. He chose to give a dollar. After reading *The Treasure Principle,* I asked, 'If I were to raise your allowance to six dollars a week, how would you use the extra dollar?' He immediately said, 'I would give two dollars.' This is just a small part of what is going on in our household."

My favorite letters are from young people, such as this one: "I am twelve years old. *The Treasure Principle* encouraged me to give at my church every week. It helped me learn that God owns everything and I just take care of it. It helped me to give more and not spend as much on things I don't need."

Responses describing the far-reaching joy from the adventure of giving are especially gratifying. Some write of large-scale life changes, including selling their real estate, jewelry, and collections, and giving the proceeds to missions.

They express deep thanks to God for the infusion of happiness that goes far beyond all expectations.

Whether the changes have been sweeping or seemingly small, these readers have experienced what I intended this book to be mainly about: enhanced joy from giving.

Honestly, at times I've been overwhelmed by the impact. I'm profoundly aware that anything God has done through *The Treasure Principle* is a work of grace on His part, and to His glory. I know without a doubt that He has used the God-breathed Scripture highlighted throughout the book to joyfully transform hearts.

I'm grateful, too, that all the book royalties have been and will continue to be given away to further God's kingdom. If my wife, Nanci, and I didn't personally know the unrivaled joy of giving, I wouldn't have been able to write *The Treasure Principle.*

To revise a work that many people have said changed their lives is daunting. I am adjusting a book that has traveled farther and wider than perhaps any work I've ever written, with the possible exception of *Heaven.* What if my revision reduces, rather than enhances, the book's power? But by making clearer some parts that readers occasionally have misunderstood, I hope I've made it better. My prayer is that the revision, which includes the all-new chapter "Was Jesus Really Talking About Financial Giving?" and a Q&A section, helps both new and old readers.

I also want to thank again my wonderful wife, Nanci, who has walked this path of giving with me. Our hearts are filled with gratefulness to God for all He is and all He has given. We thank Him for all He empowers His people to give for the good of others, for the good of the giver, and for the glory of the ultimate Giver:

"But who am I, and who are my people, that we should be able to give as generously as this? Everything comes from you, and we have given you only what comes from your hand" (1 Chronicles 29:14).

Randy Alcorn

Introduction

All your life, you've been on a treasure hunt. You've been searching for a perfect person and a perfect place. If you're a Christian, you've already met that person—Jesus. And you're headed to that place—Heaven.

But there's a problem. You're not yet living with Him in that place!

If you've asked Jesus Christ to forgive your sins, He's rescued you from eternal condemnation and given you new life. Your salvation isn't dependent on anything you have done or will ever do. Rather, it's God's gift to you, secured by Christ's death and resurrection. This is the Gospel, the "good news of happiness" (Isaiah 52:7, ESV), the "good news of great joy" (Luke 2:10, ESV).

Being saved from your sins is not about you giving to God; it's about *God giving to you.*

If you don't know Him, placing your faith in Jesus is the best choice you can ever make. By God's empowering grace, I pray you'll do it soon.

However, it's possible you already have a relationship with Jesus but feel you aren't experiencing the joy God intends. Maybe you attend church regularly, pray, and read the Bible. But life can still be drudgery, can't it? You dutifully put one foot in front of the other, plodding across the hot, barren ground, longing for an elusive joy you can't seem to find. You sense something is missing, but you don't know what.

Jesus addressed that missing element when He told a story about a hidden treasure that, once discovered, brings life-changing joy. But before we start on our journey, I want you to know something. Some books try to motivate giving out of guilt. This isn't one of them.

This book is about something else—the joy of giving. The Treasure Principle has long been buried. It's time to unearth this simple yet profound idea—one with radical implications. Once you grasp it and put it into practice, nothing will ever look the same. And you won't want it to.

When you discover the secret joy of the Treasure Principle, I guarantee you'll never be content with less.

I

Buried Treasure

He is no fool who gives what he cannot keep to gain that which he cannot lose.

JIM ELLIOT

A first-century Hebrew walks alone on a hot afternoon, staff in hand. His shoulders are stooped, his tunic stained with sweat. But he doesn't stop to rest. He has pressing business in the city.

He veers off the road into a field, seeking a shortcut. The owner won't mind—travelers are permitted this courtesy. The field is uneven. To keep his balance he thrusts his staff into the dirt.

Thunk. The staff strikes something hard.

He stops, wipes his brow, and pokes again.

Thunk. Something's under there, and it's not a rock. The weary traveler's curiosity wins out. He jabs at the ground. Something reflects a sliver of sunlight. He drops to his knees and starts digging.

Five minutes later, he's uncovered a case fringed in gold.

By the looks of it, it's been there for decades. Hands shaking and heart racing, he pries off the lock and opens the lid.

Gold coins! Jewelry! Precious stones! A treasure more valuable than anything he's ever imagined.

Some wealthy man must have buried the treasure and died suddenly, its secret location dying with him. There's no homestead nearby. Surely the current landowner has no clue this ancient treasure is here.

The traveler buries the chest and marks the spot. He turns to head home—only now he's not plodding. He's skipping like a child and smiling broadly.

What a find! Unbelievable! I've got to have that treasure! But I can't just take it. By law, whoever buys a field assumes ownership of all that's in it. But how can I afford to buy it? I'll sell my farm . . . and crops . . . all my tools . . . my prize oxen. Yes, if I sell everything, that should be enough!

From the moment of his discovery, the traveler's life changes. The treasure captures his imagination. It's his reference point, his new center of gravity. The traveler takes every new step with this treasure in mind. He experiences a radical paradigm shift.

This story is captured by Jesus in a single verse: "The kingdom of heaven is like treasure hidden in a field. When a man found it, he hid it again, and then in his joy went and sold all he had and bought that field" (Matthew 13:44).

Some believe this passage speaks of people finding the

treasure of Christ. Many believe it speaks of Jesus giving His life to obtain the treasure of the people and kingdom He rules. In either case, it certainly portrays the joy of finding eternal treasure with value that far surpasses the costs to obtain it.

THE MONEY CONNECTION

The parable of hidden treasure is one of many references Jesus made to money and possessions. In fact, 15 percent of everything Christ said relates to this topic—more than His teachings on Heaven and Hell combined.

Why did Jesus put such an emphasis on money and possessions?

Because there's a fundamental connection between our spiritual lives and how we think about and handle money. We may try to divorce our faith and finances, but God sees them as inseparable.

I came to this realization years ago while reading Luke 3 on an airplane. Among the crowds that gathered to hear John the Baptist preach, three different groups asked him how they should prove their repentance. John gave three answers:

1. Everyone should share clothes and food with the poor (v. 11).
2. Tax collectors shouldn't pocket extra money (v. 13).

3. Soldiers should be content with their wages and not extort money (v. 14).

No one had asked John about finances! They wanted to know how to demonstrate spiritual transformation. So why did John's response center almost exclusively on money and possessions?

Sitting on that plane, I realized something John wanted his audience to know: *Our approach to money and possessions is central to our spiritual lives.*

Soon that truth jumped out at me in other passages. Zacchaeus said to Jesus, "Look, Lord! Here and now I give half of my possessions to the poor, and if I have cheated anybody out of anything, I will pay back four times the amount" (Luke 19:8).

Jesus responded, "Today salvation has come to this house" (v. 9). Zacchaeus's new approach to money proved his heart had been transformed.

Acts tells of Jerusalem converts who eagerly sold their possessions to give to the needy (2:45; 4:32–35). Ephesian occultists proved the authenticity of their conversion when they burned their magic books, worth millions of dollars in today's currency (19:19).

The poor widow steps off the pages of Scripture by giving two small coins. Jesus praised her: "She out of her poverty has put in everything she had" (Mark 12:44, esv).

In stark contrast, Jesus spoke of a rich man who spent all his wealth on himself. He planned to store up for early retirement and easy living.

But God called the man a fool (Luke 12:20). The greatest indictment against him—and the proof of his spiritual condition—is that he was rich toward himself but not rich toward God.

When a rich young man pressed Jesus about how to gain eternal life, Jesus told him, "Sell your possessions and give to the poor, and you will have treasure in heaven. Then come, follow me" (Matthew 19:21). Jesus knew the man couldn't serve God until he dethroned his money idol.

But the seeker considered the price too great. Sadly, he chose lesser and fading treasures, walking away from greater and lasting ones.

Smart or Stupid?

The rich young man wasn't willing to give up everything for a greater treasure, but our traveler in the field was. Why? Because the traveler understood what he would gain.

Do you feel sorry for the traveler? After all, his discovery cost him everything. No, we aren't to pity this man; we're to *envy* him! His sacrifice pales in comparison to his reward. The cost-benefit ratio is compelling!

The traveler made short-term sacrifices to obtain a long-term reward. "It cost him everything he owned," you might lament. Yes, *but he gained far more than he lost.*

If we miss the phrase "in his joy," we miss everything. The man wasn't exchanging lesser treasures for greater treasures out of dutiful drudgery but out of joyful exhilaration.

In this parable Jesus is appealing to what we *do* value—temporary, earthly treasure—in order to make an analogy about what we *should* value—eternal, heavenly treasure. We should think of the treasure hidden in the field in Matthew 13 as representing the true and lasting treasures we find in Jesus, the gospel, and God's eternal kingdom. Any earthly treasure we part with to obtain that far greater treasure is well worth the exchange!

In Matthew 6, Jesus fully unveils the foundation of what I call the Treasure Principle. It's one of His most neglected and misinterpreted teachings:

> Do not store up for yourselves treasures on earth, where moth and rust destroy, and where thieves break in and steal. But store up for yourselves treasures in heaven, where moth and rust do not destroy, and where thieves do not break in and steal. For where your treasure is, there your heart will be also. (vv. 19–21)

Jesus says: "Do not store up for yourselves treasures on earth." Why? Because earthly treasures are bad? No. *Because they won't last.*

Scripture says, "Cast but a glance at riches, and they are gone, for they will surely sprout wings and fly off to the sky like an eagle" (Proverbs 23:5). Next time you buy a prized possession, imagine it sprouting wings and flying off. Sooner or later it *will* disappear.

When Jesus warns us not to store up treasures on Earth, it's not because wealth *might* be lost; it's because wealth will *always* be lost. Either it leaves us while we live, or we leave it when we die. No exceptions.

Imagine yourself near the end of the Civil War. You're a Northerner, stranded in the South by the war. You plan to move home when the war is over. While in the South, you've accumulated lots of Confederate currency. Suppose you know for a fact that the North is going to win the war soon. *What will you do with your Confederate money?*

If you're smart, you'll immediately cash in your excess Confederate currency for US currency—the only money that will have value after the war. You'll keep only enough Confederate currency to meet your short-term needs.

As a Christian, you have inside knowledge of an eventual worldwide upheaval caused by Christ's return. This is the ultimate insider trading tip: Earth's currency will become worthless when Christ returns—or when you die, whichever comes first. (And either event could happen at any time.)

Investment experts known as market timers read signs that the stock market is about to take a downward turn, then recommend switching funds immediately into more dependable vehicles such as money markets, treasury bills, or certificates of deposit.

Jesus functions here as the foremost market timer. He instructs us to transfer our funds from the fallen Earth (which is ready to take a permanent dive) to Heaven (which is insured by God and will soon replace Earth's economy—forever).

Though Christ's financial forecast for Earth is bleak, He's unreservedly bullish about investing in Heaven, where every market indicator is eternally positive!

Storing up earthly treasures isn't simply wrong. It's just plain stupid.

In light of the inside information revealed in Scripture, to accumulate vast earthly treasures you cannot hold on to is equivalent to stockpiling Confederate money even though you know it's about to become worthless.

According to Jesus, storing up earthly treasures isn't simply wrong. It's just plain stupid.

A Treasure Mentality

Jesus doesn't just tell us where *not* to put our treasures. He also gives the best investment advice you'll ever hear: "Store up for yourselves treasures in heaven" (Matthew 6:20).

If you stopped reading too soon, you would have thought Christ was against storing up treasures for ourselves. No, He *commands* it! Jesus *wants* us to store up treasures. He's just telling us to stop storing them in the wrong place and start storing them in the right place!

God expects us to act out of enlightened self-interest.

"Store up *for yourselves*." Doesn't it seem strange that Jesus commands us to do what's in our own best interests? Wouldn't that be selfish? No. God expects and commands us to act out of enlightened self-interest. He wants us to live to His glory, but what is to His glory is always to our good. As John Piper put it, "God is most glorified in us when we are most satisfied in Him."[2]

Selfish people pursue gain at others' expense. But God's riches are infinite. When you serve Him and others, you store up treasures in Heaven. This doesn't reduce the treasures available to others. Everyone gains; no one loses.

The man who finds the buried treasure pays a high price *now* by giving up all he has—but soon he'll gain a magnificent treasure. As long as his eyes are on that treasure, he makes his short-term sacrifices with joy. Delayed gratification lets him frontload his anticipation of future joy into present joy.

What are these "treasures in heaven"? I'll talk about that more in the next chapter. But they include godly power (Luke 19:15–19), possessions (Matthew 19:21), and pleasures (Psalm 16:11). Jesus promises that those who sacrifice on Earth will receive "a hundred times as much" in Heaven (Matthew 19:29). That's 10,000 percent—an impressive return!

Of course, Christ Himself is our ultimate treasure. All else pales in comparison to Him (Philippians 3:7–11). A person, Jesus, is our first treasure. A place, Heaven, is our second treasure. Possessions, eternal rewards, are our third treasure.

"Store up for yourselves treasures in heaven." Why? Because it's right? Not only that, but because it's *smart.* Jesus makes not an emotional appeal, but a logical one: Invest in what has lasting value.

You'll never see a hearse pulling a U-Haul. Why? *Because you can't take it with you.*

> Do not be overawed when a man grows rich,
>   when the splendor of his house increases;
> for he will take nothing with him when he dies,
>   his splendor will not descend with him.
>   (Psalm 49:16–17)

John D. Rockefeller was one of the wealthiest men who ever lived. After he died, someone asked his accountant, "How much money did John leave?" The reply was classic: "He left . . . *all* of it."

You can't take it with you.

If that point is clear in your mind, you're ready to hear the secret of the Treasure Principle.

THE TREASURE PRINCIPLE

Jesus takes that profound truth, "You can't take it with you," and adds a stunning qualification. By telling us to store up treasures for ourselves in Heaven, He gives us a remarkable corollary, which I call the Treasure Principle:

> **You can't take it with you—
> but you *can* send it on ahead.**

Anything we try to hang on to here will be lost. But anything we put into God's hands will be ours for eternity. If that doesn't take your breath away, you don't understand it!

If we invest in the eternal instead of in the temporal, we store up treasures in Heaven that will never stop paying dividends. Whatever treasures we store up on Earth will be left behind when we leave. Whatever treasures we store up in Heaven will be waiting for us when we arrive.

Financial planners tell us, "When it comes to your money, think thirty years ahead, not three months or three years." Christ, the ultimate investment counselor, takes it further. He says, "Don't ask how your investment will be paying off in just thirty years. Ask how it will be paying off in thirty *million* years."

Suppose I offer you one thousand dollars today to spend however you want. Then suppose I give you a choice—you can either have that one thousand dollars today *or* you can have ten million dollars one year from now, then ten million more every year after that. Only a fool would take the thousand dollars today! Yet that's what we do whenever we grab onto something that will last for only a moment.

Of course, there are many good things God wants us to do with money that don't involve giving. It is essential, for instance, that we provide for our family's basic material needs (1 Timothy 5:8). But these good things are only a beginning. The money God entrusts to us is eternal investment capital. Every day is an opportunity to buy up more shares in His kingdom.

You can't take it with you, but you can send it on ahead.

If you embrace this revolutionary concept, it will change your life. As you store up treasures in Heaven, you'll gain both an immediate and an everlasting version of what that man found in the hidden treasure.

Joy!

2

Was Jesus Really Talking About Financial Giving?

Store up for yourselves treasures in heaven.

MATTHEW 6:20

I've written this new chapter in response to claims that Jesus wasn't talking about financial giving when He told us to store up treasures in Heaven.

If you're already confident He was speaking about giving, you could skip to the next chapter to ponder what's at the heart of this book: the joy of giving.

But if you're even slightly uncertain about what Jesus meant by storing up treasures in Heaven, please continue reading. I think you'll be glad you did.

Jesus said, "Do not store up for yourselves treasures on earth" (Matthew 6:19). The parable of the rich fool in Luke 12:13–21 demonstrates the consequences for those who ignore His command. God says to the self-centered, materialistic man, "'Fool! This night your soul is required of you, and the things you have prepared, whose will they be?' So is the one who lays up treasure for himself and is not rich toward God" (vv. 20–21, ESV).

This is an uncomfortable message, but it's certainly not unclear. Storing up treasures for yourself on Earth means hanging on to money and possessions rather than generously sharing them.

But what does Jesus mean when He tells us, "Store up for yourselves treasures in heaven" (Matthew 6:20)? To understand, we must grasp the meaning of two nouns, *Heaven* and *treasures,* and the Greek verb translated *store up.*

WHAT IS HEAVEN?

Heaven is the location of God's throne, the place from which He governs the universe, where He dwells with His angels and His people who have died. The present Heaven will, after our bodily resurrection, be relocated to the New Earth (Revelation 21:3). That location will be the future Heaven, since it will become the center of God's ruling presence, and the location of His throne (Revelation 22:3).

Many Christians think "treasures in heaven" won't be tangible because they imagine Heaven won't be tangible. But the future Heaven, on the New Earth, will not be an intangible state where we float about as disembodied spirits. On the contrary, as I develop in my book *Heaven,* it will be a real, material place.

On God's New Earth, "His servants will serve him" (Revelation 22:3). Servants always have things to do, places to go, and people to see. We will worship God, and we will eat, drink, celebrate, laugh, rest, work, and play together as physical people in a physical world.

(By the way, I capitalize Heaven because it's a proper noun, a place every bit as real as the town you live in. The New Earth will be as real as New England, so it deserves capitalization too.)

WHAT ARE TREASURES IN HEAVEN?

The Greek word translated "treasures" or "riches" in Matthew 6 normally means "accumulated wealth in the form of money, jewels, or other valuables."[3] That's exactly what Christ's disciples would have immediately thought of: tangible wealth, valuable assets, precious possessions.

It's true that when Jesus speaks about "treasures in heaven," we don't know the exact form those treasures will take. Treasures in Heaven could be of material or spiritual nature, but either way they are real, meaningful rewards for God's people who give generously.

In Matthew 6, Jesus tells us to transfer our wealth from one place to another. When we die, earthly treasure will no longer be ours, but wealth we've transferred to Heaven will remain ours forever.

God will also give us eternal rewards for doing good works (Ephesians 6:8; Romans 2:6, 10), persevering under persecution (Luke 6:22–23), showing compassion to the needy (Luke 14:13–14), and treating our enemies kindly (Luke 6:35).

We're told that "the saints of the Most High shall receive the kingdom and possess the kingdom forever, forever and ever" (Daniel 7:18, ESV). What is "the kingdom"? Earth. On the New Earth, God's children will reign with Christ (Revelation 20:6). Faithful servants will be put "in charge of many things" (Matthew 25:21, 23).

Scripture refers to five different crowns, which may or may not be literal but clearly represent actual ruling positions in God's kingdom. Treasures in Heaven, then, will surely include the rewards of God entrusting His faithful children with positions of leadership in proportion to their service on Earth (Luke 19:12–19).

Once we grasp what Heaven really is and will be, we can begin to understand what Christ meant when He talked about storing up treasures there.

How Can We Store Up Treasures in Heaven?

Jesus explicitly said that God will grant us rewards for generous giving: "Go, sell your possessions and give to the poor, and you will have treasure in heaven" (Matthew 19:21).

It seemed obvious to me when I first wrote *The Treasure Principle* that Christ's words here are directly parallel to what He said in Matthew 6:19–21 about storing up treasures in Heaven. However, several people, including some reviewers of this book, have claimed that Jesus wasn't talking about financial giving.

Since I reference many other foundational biblical passages, even if Matthew 6 doesn't refer to giving, it wouldn't invalidate the whole book. But it would certainly mean the book is poorly named and that I should correct my misinterpretation.

So, when Jesus spoke about storing up treasures in Heaven, was He really talking about giving away our earthly treasures to help the needy?

My answer is yes, for three reasons: (1) the immediate context, (2) the clear wording of Matthew 19:21, and (3) two more parallel passages in the other Gospels and one of Paul's letters. These make it emphatically clear that giving away money and possessions is *exactly* what Jesus was talking about.

Shortly before speaking about treasures on Earth and in Heaven, Jesus told His disciples in Matthew 6:1–4 not to seek human reward for their financial giving, for then "you will have no reward from your Father in heaven." He added that if they do their giving (and in the following verses, their prayer and fasting) for God and not for men to see, "your Father, who sees what is done in secret, will reward you."

That's the immediate context that leads up to Jesus saying, "Store up for yourselves treasures in heaven" (v. 20).

The Greek word rendered "store up" (NIV, NASB) or "lay up" (KJV, ESV) means "to store away (valuables) for future use."[4] What are the *treasures* here? The Louw-Nida Greek Lexicon defines the original Greek word used in this verse, *thesauros,* as "that which is of exceptional value and kept safe—'treasure, wealth, riches.'"[5] (It's the same word used for the hidden treasure in Matthew 13.)

When His disciples heard Jesus speak of treasures on Earth, they would naturally have thought of money and possessions.

Jesus not only *precedes* His words about storing treasures in Heaven by referring to our motives in financial giving (6:1–4), He *follows* them by calling money another master (Matthew 6:24).

In addition, three parallel passages explicitly identify financial giving as the means to store up treasures in Heaven.

Following His parable of the rich fool, who was a keeper, not a giver, Jesus speaks of material goods, earthly treasures, telling His followers not to chase after such things. He says in Luke 12:31, "But seek his kingdom, and these things will be given to you as well."

Then He adds, "Do not be afraid, little flock, for your

Father has been pleased to give you the kingdom" (Luke 12:32). Jesus is talking about His kingdom that will be Heaven on Earth.

This leads us right to these words of Jesus: "Sell your possessions and give to the poor. Provide purses for yourselves that will not wear out, a treasure in heaven that will not be exhausted, where no thief comes near and no moth destroys. For where your treasure is, there your heart will be also" (Luke 12:33–34).

There's no ambiguity here: Taking money and possessions we could have stored up for ourselves on Earth and instead giving them to the poor is how we store up treasures in Heaven. The language of treasures, thieves, moths, and our hearts following our treasures demonstrates that the meaning of Luke 12 mirrors the meaning of Matthew 6.

Similarly, Mark quotes Jesus as saying, "Go, sell everything you have and give to the poor, and you will have treasure in heaven" (Mark 10:21).

Jesus' message is convicting *and* clear: it's all about giving and rewards for giving.

One final parallel passage comes from the apostle Paul, when he uses Christ's language in Matthew 6 to instruct Timothy what to say to the rich:

Tell them to use their money to do good. They should be rich in good works and *generous to those*

in need, always being *ready to share with others.*
By doing this they will be *storing up their treasure*
as a good foundation for the future so that they may
experience true life. (1 Timothy 6:18–19, NLT)

Just as Jesus did, Paul encourages God's people to give
their temporal treasures to those in need, realizing that
greater treasures will await us in Heaven.

CONCLUSION

As we've seen, there's overwhelming interpretive evidence as
to the meaning of Matthew 6:19–21, not just in its immediate context, but also in the parallel passages in Matthew 19;
Mark 10; Luke 12; and 1 Timothy 6. Together, they confirm
that storing up treasures in Heaven means giving generously
to kingdom causes and receiving God's rewards for doing so.

Unfortunately, some commentaries and several sermons
I've heard and read on Matthew 6:19–21 are remarkably
vague as to its meaning. They spiritualize the passage, di-
vorcing it from its context and failing to connect it to its
parallel passages. They interpret Christ's words as a general
call to be kingdom-minded and say He makes no reference
to giving away material goods.

Certainly the passage would be far easier to fulfill if it
merely required good intentions on our part. Instead, it calls

us to radical acts of generosity. We dare not let our convenience and culture—including church culture—dictate our interpretation.

Craig Blomberg states in the New American Commentary on Matthew, "In this context . . . storing up treasures focuses particularly on the compassionate use of material resources to meet others' physical and spiritual needs, in keeping with the priorities of God's kingdom."[6]

Of course, Christ's words can be broadly applied to how we use our time and abilities. But we must not deny or neglect His primary meaning concerning giving away our money and possessions.

Having established that when He told us to store up treasures in Heaven Jesus *was* talking about financial giving, let's now look at the matchless joy God promises when we give!

3

Compounding Joy

*The less I spent on myself and the more
I gave away, the fuller of happiness
and blessing did my soul become.*

HUDSON TAYLOR

In 1990, I was a pastor of a large church, making a good salary and earning book royalties. I had been a pastor for thirteen years, and I didn't want to do anything else.

Then our family's life was turned upside down. I was on the board of a pregnancy resource center, and we had opened our home to a pregnant teenager, helping her place her baby for adoption in a Christian home. We also had the joy of seeing her come to faith in Christ.

After searching Scripture and praying, I began participating in peaceful, nonviolent civil disobedience at abortion clinics. We simply stood in front of the doors to advocate on behalf of unborn children scheduled to die.

For this I was arrested and sent to jail. An abortion clinic won a court judgment against a group of us. I told a judge that I would pay anything I owed, but I couldn't hand over money to people who would use it to kill babies.

(Please understand, I've never failed to pay other debts. But I could not voluntarily pay money to a business that existed to kill children. I chose to live with the legal consequences of refusing to do so.)

Then I discovered my church would be forced to surrender one-fourth of my wages each month to the abortion clinic. The church would have to either pay the abortion clinic or defy a court order. To prevent this, I resigned.

That judgment was one of the best things that ever happened to us.

I'd already divested myself of book royalties. The only way I could avoid garnishment was to make no more than minimum wage. Fortunately, our family had been living on only a portion of my church salary, and we had just made our final house payment.

Another court judgment followed, involving another abortion clinic. Though our actions had been nonviolent, the clinic was awarded the largest judgment ever against a group of peaceful protestors: $8.2 million. It seemed likely we would lose our house.

By all appearances, our lives had taken a devastating turn. Right?

Wrong. That judgment was one of the best things that ever happened to us.

What others intended for evil, God intended for good (Genesis 50:20). We began a new ministry. My wife, Nanci, worked at a secretary's salary, supplementing my minimum wage. Her name alone was on all our assets, including the house. My inability to legally own assets was nothing I sought after, but God used it to help me understand what He means by "Everything under heaven belongs to me" (Job 41:11).

This wasn't the first time God taught me about His ownership. Many years ago, I had a new portable stereo, back when those were cool. I loaned it to our church's high school group for a retreat. It was returned beat-up and, I admit, it bothered me. But the Lord reminded me it wasn't *my* stereo—it was His. And it had been used to help reach young people. Who was I to complain?

Back then the material possessions I valued most were my thousands of books. I loaned them out, but it troubled me when they weren't returned or came back looking shabby.

Then I sensed God's leading to hand over all the books to begin a church library. I later looked at the names of those who checked them out, sometimes dozens of names per book. I smiled, realizing that by releasing the books, I had invested in others' lives. Suddenly, the more worn the book, the happier it made me. My perspective totally changed.

God used stereos and books and court judgments to take my understanding of His ownership to a new level. Contemplate His words:

- The earth is the LORD's, and everything in it. The world and all its people belong to him. (Psalm 24:1, NLT)
- "The silver is mine and the gold is mine," declares the LORD Almighty. (Haggai 2:8)
- Remember the LORD your God, for it is he who gives you the ability to produce wealth. (Deuteronomy 8:18)
- You are not your own; you were bought at a price. (1 Corinthians 6:19–20)

God was teaching me the first of six keys to understanding the Treasure Principle:

God is the owner of everything, including books and stereos, houses and cars, clothes and jewelry, electronics and toys. He even owns me and you, our souls and our bodies. God never revoked His ownership, never surrendered His claim to all treasures.

TREASURE PRINCIPLE KEY #1

God owns everything. I'm His money manager.

Ironically, the same year I first engaged in civil disobedience, 1989, I'd written extensively about God's ownership in my book *Money, Possessions, and Eternity.* By the time the book came out, I no longer legally owned anything. God revealed to me, in the crucible of adversity, the life-changing implications of that truth.

I realized our house belonged to God, not us. Why worry about whether or not we would keep it? He could easily provide us another place to live.

But understanding ownership was only half my lesson. If God was the owner, I was the manager. I needed to adopt a steward's mentality toward the assets He had entrusted— not given—to me.

A steward manages assets for the owner's benefit. He carries no sense of entitlement to the assets he manages. It's his job to find out what the owner wants done with his assets, then to carry out his will.

JOYFUL GIVING

Jerry Caven had a successful restaurant chain, two banks, a ranch, a farm, and real estate ventures. At age fifty-nine, he was searching for a lakeside retirement home. But the Owner had other plans.

"God led us to put our money and time overseas," Jerry says. "It's been exciting. Before, we gave token amounts.

Now we put substantial money into missions. We often go to India."

What changed the Cavens' attitude toward giving?

"It was realizing God's ownership," Jerry explains. "Once we understood that we were giving away God's money to do God's work, we discovered a peace and joy we never had back when we thought it was our money!"

One day a distraught man rode his horse up to John Wesley (1703–1791), shouting, "Mr. Wesley, something terrible happened! Your house burned to the ground!"

Wesley weighed the news, then calmly replied, "No. The *Lord's* house burned to the ground. That means one less responsibility for me."

Wesley's reaction wasn't denial. Rather, it was a bold affirmation of God's ownership.

Whenever we think like owners, it's a red flag. We should be thinking like stewards, investment managers, always looking for the best place to invest the Owner's money. One day we'll undergo a job performance evaluation: "For we will all stand before God's judgment seat. . . . So then, each of us will give an account of himself to God" (Romans 14:10, 12).

Our name is on God's account. We have unrestricted access to it. As His money managers, God trusts us to set our own salaries. We draw needed funds from His wealth to pay our living expenses. One of our central spiritual decisions is determining a reasonable amount to live on. Whatever that amount is—and it will legitimately vary from person to person—we shouldn't hoard or indiscriminately spend the excess. After all, it's His, not ours.

Every spring my wife and I read through dozens of letters from people in our church who are going on summer missions trips and asking for support. (One year we received forty-five requests.) When this time comes each year, we feel like kids in a candy store—a store as big as the world and as expansive as the heart of God.

Why such excitement?

Because we get to invest in our brothers and sisters in Christ who are sharing the Gospel. We get to hear stories and read e-mails about what God is doing in many different countries.

We see the enthusiasm, the growth, the kingdom-mindedness, the changed priorities of people young and old. We pray that those who go—and those to whom they go—will never be the same. And we will have had a part in it!

I attended a gathering of givers where we took turns telling our stories. The words *fun, joy, exciting,* and *wonderful* kept surfacing. There were lots of smiles, laughter, and tears of joy. One older couple shared how they travel around the world, participating in the ministries they give to. Meanwhile, their home is becoming run-down. They said, "Our children tell us, 'Fix up your house or buy a new one. You can afford it.' We tell them, 'Why would we do that? That's not what excites us!'"

Ray Berryman, CEO for a national municipal services firm, says he and his wife give at least half of their income to God's work each year. "My joy in giving comes from serving God in a way that I know He's called me to and realizing that what I give is impacting people for Christ," Ray says. "It's exciting to know we're part of evangelizing, discipling, helping, and feeding the needy. It just feels wonderful."

The more we give, the more we delight in our giving. It pleases us. But more important, it pleases God.

"God loves a cheerful giver" (2 Corinthians 9:7). However, the cheerfulness often comes during and after the act of obedience, not before it. So don't wait until you feel like giving! Just give and watch the joy follow.

God wants us to find joy. He even *commands* us to rejoice (Philippians 4:4). But if we don't give, we're robbed of an important source of the joy God instructs us to seek!

I know a single man who came to Christ in his twenties, read the Scriptures, and got so excited that he decided to sell his house and give the money to God. But when he shared this plan with his Bible-study group, something tragic happened: they talked him out of it.

Over the years, I've heard from readers who say they believe the group's counsel saved this young man from an unwise decision. I disagree, largely because I knew his circumstances and the depth of his conviction and his joy at the prospect of doing this. He was highly skilled with a well-paying job.

Had he sold his house and given away the profits, instead of being in the 99th percentile of the world's wealthy, he might have dropped to the 98th percentile. But he would have had both treasures in Heaven and the joy of knowing he had followed the Lord's prompting to help others. It would likely have set his life on a trajectory of trust in God instead of conformity to the usual way of doing things. To this day I wonder what great things God might have done through this young man had he not been talked out of doing what he believed God wanted him to do.

When it comes to money and possessions, the cultures of the world and the church sometimes seem indistinguishable. If you ever feel inclined to talk a young believer (including your child) out of giving, please restrain yourself. Don't quench God's Spirit, and don't rob someone of present joy and future rewards. Instead, watch and learn. Then ask God what He wants *you* to give away, and what gladness He wants to bring into *your* life.

THUNDER, LIGHTNING, AND GRACE

The Macedonian Christians understood the joy of giving: "Out of the most severe trial, their overflowing joy and their extreme poverty welled up in rich generosity" (2 Corinthians 8:2).

How do "severe trial," "overflowing joy," "extreme poverty," and "rich generosity" all fit in one verse? Giving isn't a luxury of the rich. It's a joyous privilege of the poor. I've discovered that impoverished Christians in many countries find great joy in giving.

The Macedonians, according to Paul, "urgently pleaded with us for the privilege of sharing in this service to the saints" (v. 4). They had to plead, presumably because others were telling them that their poverty exempted them from giving.

> *Giving isn't a luxury of the rich. It's a joyous privilege of the poor.*

These early Christians were dirt-poor but came up with every reason they could to give. What a contrast to those who have so much but come up with endless justifications for *not* giving!

It's humbling to receive gifts from people in far greater need than you. I've experienced this on missions trips where the poor gladly serve their best food to visiting Americans. They're not pretending their sacrifice makes them happy. It *really* does.

When the tabernacle was being built, people were so excited they had to be "restrained" from giving more (Exodus 36:5–7). That's what giving will do to you.

God uses giving to conform us to His image. Gaze upon Christ long enough and you'll become more of a giver. Give long enough and you'll become more like Christ.

Paul says in 2 Corinthians 8:1: "We want you to know about the grace that God has given the Macedonian churches." How was God's grace demonstrated? By their act of giving to needy Christians. In verse 6, Paul calls the Macedonians' giving to help the hungry in Jerusalem an "act of grace." The same Greek word is used for Christian *giving* and for God's *grace.*

Christ's grace defines, motivates, and puts in perspective our giving: "For you know the grace of our Lord Jesus Christ, that though he was rich, yet for your sakes he became poor, so that you through his poverty might become rich" (v. 9).

Contemplate Christ's giving of Himself on our behalf. The infinitely wealthy King chose to become poor, not only to save us from Hell, but also to make us rich by buying our peace with God through His own death. God's grace is His giving to us in Christ the righteousness He loves and we desperately need, while taking in exchange our sin that He hates and which we need deliverance from.

Our giving is a reflexive response to God's grace in our lives. It doesn't come out of our altruism or philanthropy for which we might congratulate ourselves. Rather, it comes out of Christ's transforming work in us. We give because He first gave to us. While our giving to Him pales in comparison to His giving to us, it pleases God when we follow His example.

The greatest passage on giving in all Scripture ends not with "Congratulations for your generosity," but with "Thanks be to God for his indescribable gift!" (2 Corinthians 9:15).

When God's grace touches us, we give joyfully.

As thunder follows lightning, joyful giving follows grace. When the lightning of God's grace strikes us, the thunder of our giving should follow. When we're not givers, it means we're not being permeated by His grace and the joy that's inseparable from it.

THE FRINGE BENEFITS OF GIVING

Mark, an attorney, gives away half his income each year. "My pursuit of money drove me away from God," Mark says. "But since I've been giving it to Him, everything's changed. Giving has brought me closer to God than anything else."

In the movie *Chariots of Fire*, Olympian Eric Liddell is portrayed as saying, "I believe God made me for a purpose. . . . And when I run, I feel His pleasure." Those who've discovered the Treasure Principle will testify, "When I give, I feel His pleasure."

There have been days when I've lost focus, and then a need arises and God leads me to give. Suddenly I'm infused with energy, purpose, and joy. I feel God's pleasure. Giving is therapy, not just for the receiver, but also for the giver.

God said, "I give to the Levites as their inheritance the tithes that the Israelites present as an offering to the LORD" (Numbers 18:24). It may have looked like the people were giving to their spiritual leaders, but they actually gave to God, and He designated His funds to the Levites. Christians should love their pastors and support them financially (Galatians 6:6), but first and foremost we give to God (2 Corinthians 8:5) as an act of worship.

Giving jump-starts our relationship with God. It opens our fists so we can receive what God has for us. When we see what it does for others and for us, we open our fists sooner and wider when the next chance comes.

Proverbs 21:13 tells us, "If a man shuts his ears to the cry of the poor, he too will cry out and not be answered." In Isaiah 58:6–10, God says that His willingness to answer our prayers is directly affected by whether we're caring for the needy and oppressed. Want to empower your prayer life? Give.

It was said of Josiah, "'He defended the cause of the poor and needy, and so all went well. Is that not what it means to know me?' declares the LORD" (Jeremiah 22:16). Caring for the needy flows out of knowing God, and draws us closer to Him.

(The world is also full of the spiritually needy, the lost

who are impoverished by not having heard the gospel of Jesus and/or not having access to God's Word in their native languages. Hence, we're also helping the needy whenever we give to world evangelism and church planting.)

Giving brings freedom. It's a matter of physics. The greater the mass, the greater the hold that mass exerts. The more things we own—the greater their total mass—the more they pull us into orbit around them. Finally, like a black hole, they suck us in.

Giving breaks us out of the orbit around our possessions. We escape their gravity, entering a new orbit around Heaven, the residence of our King Jesus, where we've invested our treasures.

WHAT CHRISTIANS CAN LEARN
FROM GENEROUS UNBELIEVERS

All people are made in God's likeness. By His common grace, Christ followers aren't the only ones who can discover enormous joy in giving.

Speaking of world needs, novelist Stephen King wrote, "We have the power to help, the power to change. And why should we refuse? Because we're going to take it with us? Please."

He continued, sharing sort of a secular version of the Treasure Principle: "I want you to consider making your lives one long gift to others, and why not? All you have is on loan, anyway. . . . All that lasts is what you pass on."[7]

Investor T. Boone Pickens talked about how good it feels to give. He said, "I was put here to make money so I could give it away."[8]

I heard a nearly giddy Warren Buffet, then the second or third richest person in the world, say he once wondered why he'd made billions of dollars. Then he said he'd discovered the reason: so he can help many people. Buffet created the Giving Pledge, which at this writing has been signed by 156 billionaires who've joined him in committing to give away most of their wealth.

Bill Gates said, "I've accelerated my philanthropic plans. Melinda and I are convinced that there are certain kinds of gifts—investments in the future—that are better made sooner than later."[9] He also said, "A fortune . . . is best not passed on to one's children. It's not constructive for them."[10]

Actress Angelina Jolie said, "If I decide to go visit a school in the middle of Kenya, or Russia, the kids will be excited. That's better than having an Oscar. . . . When I'm in a refugee camp, my spirit feels better there than anywhere else in the world . . . they don't know who I am. I am useful as a woman who's willing to spend a day in the dirt."[11] Sharing about her humanitarian work, she said, "Second to my children, spending time with refugees and other persons of need around the world has been the greatest gift."[12]

For every megawealthy person who's discovered the joy of giving, thousands more with low to middle incomes have discovered the same. Their names aren't known outside their communities, but they're touching countless lives worldwide.

Many people, rich and poor, who don't personally know Christ and have never been transformed by God's grace, have discovered profound happiness in giving. Shouldn't we who are Christ's followers have learned a great deal more? Yet, sadly, I meet many Christians who still haven't been captivated by the joy of giving. (The good news is, it's not too late!)

GIVING AS AN INCREDIBLE PRIVILEGE

Despite the $8.2 million court judgment twenty-six years ago, we never lost our house. While paying me a minimum-wage salary, the ministry received all the royalties from my books. With joy in our hearts, Nanci and I continue giving away 100 percent of the book royalties to missions, ministries, famine relief, and pro-life work. When we first started doing this in 1989, book royalties began to dramatically increase.

Since Eternal Perspective Ministries (EPM) began, by God's grace, the ten million books sold have brought in over eight million dollars of royalties. I try to write good, biblically based books, but sometimes I think God sells those books mainly to raise funds for ministries and people close to His heart!

Some have wondered if I realize what we could have done with eight million dollars. My answer is always the same: Nothing that would have brought us nearly as much joy as we've found in giving it away.

There's just nothing like giving. It's exhilarating. For me, the only feeling that compares is the joy of leading someone to Christ. The great thing is that our giving to missions helps people come to Christ all over the world. Someday we'll meet them in Heaven! When that happens, will any of us wish we'd kept that money instead of giving it?

You could never pay givers enough to convince them not to give.

Giving brings us far more than it takes. It infuses our lives with gladness and gratitude. It interjects an eternal dimension into the most ordinary day. That's one reason you could never pay givers enough to convince them not to give.

But hold on—great as it is, our present joy isn't the best part of the Treasure Principle.

4

Eyes on Eternity

For the Son of Man is going to come in his Father's glory with his angels, and then he will reward each person according to what he has done.

Matthew 16:27

The streets of Cairo were hot and dusty. Our missionary friends Pat and Rakel Thurman took us down an alley. We drove past Arabic signs to an overgrown graveyard for American missionaries.

As Nanci and I and our daughters, Karina and Angela, followed, Pat pointed to a sun-scorched tombstone that read: "William Borden 1887–1913."

Borden, a Yale graduate and heir to great wealth, rejected a life of ease in order to bring the gospel to Muslims. Refusing even to buy himself a car, Borden gave away hundreds of thousands of dollars to missions. After only four months of zealous ministry in Egypt, he contracted spinal meningitis and died at age twenty-five.

I dusted off the epitaph on Borden's grave. After describing his love for God and sacrifices for Muslim people, the inscription ended with a phrase I've never forgotten: "Apart from faith in Christ, there is no explanation for such a life."

The Thurmans took us from Borden's grave to the Egyptian Museum. The King Tut exhibit was mind-boggling.

Tutankhamun died at age seventeen. He was buried with solid gold chariots and thousands of golden artifacts. His gold coffin was found buried within gold tombs within gold tombs.

The ancient Egyptians believed in an afterlife—one where they could take earthly treasures. But all the treasures intended for King Tut's eternal enjoyment stayed right where they were for more than three thousand years, until Howard Carter discovered the burial chamber in 1922.

I was struck by the contrast between these two graves. Borden's was obscure, dusty, and hidden off a back street littered with garbage. Tutankhamun's tomb glittered with unimaginable wealth. Yet where are these two men now? One, who lived in opulence and called himself king, is in the misery of a Christless eternity. The other, who lived a modest life in service of the one true King, is enjoying everlasting reward in his Lord's presence.

Tut's life was tragic because of an awful truth discovered too late—he couldn't take his treasures with him. William Borden's life was triumphant. Why? Because instead of leaving behind his treasures, he sent them on ahead.

ETERNAL REWARDS

If you imagine Heaven as a place where you will strum a harp in endless tedium, you probably dread it. But if you trust Scripture, you will be filled with anticipation for your heavenly home. Heaven will be a place of rest and relief from sin and suffering; but it will also be a place of great learning, activity, artistic expression, exploration, camaraderie, and service.[13]

Jesus notices our smallest acts of kindness: "If anyone gives even a cup of cold water to one of these little ones because he is my disciple, I tell you the truth, he will certainly not lose his reward" (Matthew 10:42).

God keeps a record of all we do for Him: "A scroll of remembrance was written in his presence concerning those who feared the LORD and honored his name" (Malachi 3:16).

Imagine a scribe in Heaven recording each of your gifts. The bike you gave to the neighbor kid, the books to prisoners, the monthly donations to the church, missionaries, and pregnancy center—all are being chronicled. Scrolls are made to be read. I look forward to hearing your giving stories and meeting those touched by what you gave.

Jesus said, "If you have not been trustworthy in handling worldly wealth, who will trust you with true riches?" (Luke 16:11). If you handle His money faithfully, Christ will give you true, eternal riches.

After speaking of the shrewd servant's desire to use earthly resources so that "people will welcome me into their houses" (Luke 16:4), Jesus told His followers to use "worldly wealth" (money and possessions) to "gain friends" (by making a difference in their lives on Earth). The reason? "So that when it is gone [when life on Earth is over], you will be welcomed into eternal dwellings" (v. 9).

Our "friends" in Heaven will be those whose lives we've touched on Earth, who will have their own "eternal dwellings." Luke 16:9 seems to say our friends' eternal dwellings are places where we stay and fellowship, perhaps as we move about the heavenly kingdom. The money we give to help others on Earth will open doors of fellowship in Heaven. Now *that's* something to get excited about!

John Bunyan wrote *Pilgrim's Progress* in prison. He said:

> Whatever good thing you do for Him, if done
> according to the Word, is laid up for you as treasure
> in chests and coffers, to be brought out to be rewarded
> before both men and angels, to your eternal comfort.[14]

Is this a biblical concept? Absolutely. Paul spoke about the Philippians' financial giving and explained, "Not that I am looking for a gift, but I am looking for what may be credited to your account" (Philippians 4:17). God keeps an account open for us in Heaven, and every gift given for His glory is a deposit in that account. (Have you been making regular deposits?)

Isn't It Unspiritual and Selfish to Talk About Eternal Rewards?

You cannot understand what Jesus is saying in Matthew 6:19–21 as long as you tell yourself it's wrong to value treasures. You must believe it is right to want to do what Jesus tells you to do: store up treasures *for yourself* in Heaven.

One of the most common criticisms of this book has been that believers shouldn't be motivated by personal gain but only by the desire to lose themselves for the sake of Christ.

People often tell me they think it's ungodly to want rewards. But Scripture brims with passages in which God promises rewards for our faithfulness to Him. I typically respond, "If it were wrong to want them, Christ wouldn't offer rewards as motivation. Rewards are God's idea, not ours!"

Love for God, love for people, and compassion for the poor are all vitally important. But these motives for giving are in no way contrary to the fact that God also calls us to be motivated by rewards.

Our instinct is to give to those who will give us something in return. But Jesus told us to give to "the poor, the crippled, the lame, the blind. ... Although they cannot

repay you, you will be repaid at the resurrection of the righ-
teous" (Luke 14:13–14). If we give to those who can't reward
us, Christ guarantees He will personally reward us. He's
talking about treasures that await us in Heaven, rewards for
caring for the poor, including our efforts to reach the unreached with the gospel of Jesus.

Giving is a giant lever positioned on the fulcrum of this
world, allowing us to move mountains in the next world.
Because we give, eternity will be different—for others and
for us.

A HEART IN THE RIGHT PLACE

God promises us generous heavenly rewards in a magnificent
New Heaven and New Earth free from the curse and suffering (see Revelation 21:1–6). We'll forever be with the person
we were made for, in a place made
for us.

*Many Christians
dread the thought of
leaving this world.*

Nevertheless, many Christians
dread the thought of leaving this
world.

Why? Because so many have stored up their treasures on
Earth, not in Heaven. Each day brings us closer to death. If
your treasures are on Earth, each day brings you closer to
losing them.

John Wesley toured a vast estate with a proud plantation

owner. They rode their horses for hours and saw only a fraction of the man's property. At the end of the day they sat down to dinner. The plantation owner eagerly asked, "Well, Mr. Wesley, what do you think?"

Wesley replied, "I think you're going to have a hard time leaving all this."

I spoke with Laverne, a woman with terminal cancer. Through tears she said, "It blows me away to know that God's chosen me to give. It won't be long before I see Him face to face. I just want to hear Him say, 'Well done, my good and faithful servant.'"

Suddenly, Laverne laughed. "What else matters?" she said. "Why should I care about anything else?"

Laverne's heart was focused on heavenly treasures, and the more she gave away, the more she felt ready to die. Each day brought her closer to those treasures she'd stored up in Heaven.

Jesus said, "Where your treasure is, there your heart will be also" (Matthew 6:21). That's the second key to the Treasure Principle.

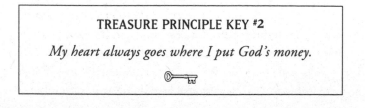

TREASURE PRINCIPLE KEY #2

My heart always goes where I put God's money.

By telling us that our hearts follow our treasure, Jesus is saying, "Show me your bank records and your Visa statement, and I'll show you where your heart is." What we do with our money doesn't simply indicate where our hearts are. According to Jesus, it *determines* where our hearts go.

Suppose you buy shares of Ford Motor Company. What happens? You suddenly develop an interest in Ford. You check the financial pages. You see a magazine article about Ford and read every word. You probably buy a Ford as your next car.

Suppose you're giving to help African children deal with AIDS. When you see an article on the subject, you're hooked. If you're sending money to plant Indian churches and an earthquake hits India, you watch the news and fervently pray. You develop a passionate interest in God's kingdom.

> *As surely as the compass needle follows north, your heart will follow your treasure.*

As surely as the compass needle follows north, your heart will follow your treasure. This is a remarkable truth. If I want my heart somewhere, all I need to do is put my money there.

I've heard people say, "I want more of a heart for missions." I always respond, "Jesus tells you exactly how to get it. Put your money in missions, and your heart will follow."

Do you wish you cared more about eternal things? Then reallocate some of your money, maybe *most* of it, from temporal to eternal things. Watch what happens. You'll be amazed . . . and happy.

God wants your heart. He isn't looking for dispassionate "philanthropists" for His kingdom. He's looking for disciples so filled with a vision for eternity that they wouldn't dream of not investing their money, time, and prayers where they will matter most.

Of course, giving isn't the only good thing we can do with money. We need to feed, clothe, house, and transport our families. But when the basics are taken care of, why shouldn't the rest go toward treasures in Heaven?

Moses left Egypt's treasures "because he was looking ahead to his reward" (Hebrews 11:26).

He who lays up treasures on Earth spends his life backing away from his treasures. To him, death is loss.

He who lays up treasures in Heaven looks forward to eternity; he's moving daily toward his treasures. To him, death is gain.

He who spends his life moving away from his treasures has reason to despair. He who spends his life moving toward his treasures has reason to rejoice.

Are you despairing or rejoicing?

5

Roadblocks
to Giving

*Be on your guard against all kinds of
greed; a man's life does not consist in the
abundance of his possessions.*

LUKE 12:15

We know that Christ commands us to give. And we know He offers us great rewards for giving. Maybe we even believe that giving brings happiness.

So why is it so hard to give?

There are many roadblocks to giving: unbelief, insecurity, pride, idolatry, desire for control. The raging current of our culture—and often our churches—makes it hard to swim upstream. It's considered "normal" to keep far more than we give.

But I'm convinced that the greatest deterrent to giving is this: the illusion that the present Earth is our home. This leads us to the next key to the Treasure Principle:

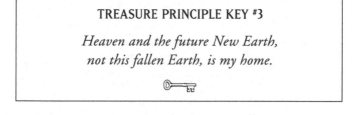

TREASURE PRINCIPLE KEY #3

Heaven and the future New Earth,
not this fallen Earth, is my home.

The Bible says we're pilgrims, strangers, aliens on Earth (Hebrews 11:13). We're ambassadors representing our true country (2 Corinthians 5:20). "Our citizenship is in heaven" (Philippians 3:20). We're citizens of "a better country—a heavenly one" (Hebrews 11:16).

Where we choose to store our treasures depends largely on where we think our home is.

Suppose your home is in America, but you're visiting France for three months, living in a hotel. You're told you can't bring anything back on your flight home. But you can earn money in France and send deposits home.

Would you fill your hotel room with expensive furniture and art? Of course not. You would spend only what you needed on the temporary residence, sending your treasures ahead so they'd be waiting for you when you got home.

Both of our daughters were married within weeks of each other. Friends and family set aside their busy schedules and traveled in from all over the country. When the King's wedding day comes, the universe will screech to a halt. The Groom from Nazareth and His beloved bride will take center stage (Revelation 19:7–9).

Every day of our lives we're traveling toward that wedding—*our* wedding! It's closer today than it was yesterday. Our Bridegroom, the Carpenter, is building a place for us in Heaven. Everything we do for Him, everything we send on ahead, will be waiting there for us.

Jesus is a builder by trade. He's also omniscient and omnipotent, qualities that come in handy on a building project! Don't you think that the home He's been building for us the last two thousand years will be incredible?

If we would let this reality sink in, it would forever change the way we think and live. We would stop laying up treasures in our earthly hotel rooms and start sending more ahead to our true home.

THE MOST TOYS

Take a ride with me. After a few miles we turn off the road, pass through a gate, and fall in line behind some pickup trucks. The vehicles ahead are filled with computers, furniture, appliances, and toys.

Higher and higher we climb, until we reach a parking lot. There the drivers unload their cargo. Curious, you watch a man hoist a television. He staggers to the corner of the lot, then hurls it over the edge.

Now you've got to find out what's going on. You scramble out of the car and peer over the precipice. At the bottom of the cliff is a giant pit filled with . . . stuff.

Finally you understand. This is a junkyard—the final resting place for the things we accumulate.

Sooner or later, everything we own ends up here. Christmas and birthday presents. Cars, boats, and hot tubs. Clothes, sound systems, computer monitors, and barbecue grills. The treasures that children quarreled about, friendships were lost over, and marriages broke up over—all end up here. (I recommend taking a family field trip to a junkyard. It's a powerful object lesson.)

We move into eternity, but our stuff stays behind.

Ever seen that bumper sticker "He who dies with the most toys wins"? Millions of people act as if it were true. The more accurate saying is "He who dies with the most toys still dies—and leaves his toys behind."

When we die after devoting our lives to acquiring things, we don't win—we lose. We move into eternity, but our stuff stays behind, filling junkyards.

I think of it in terms of a dot and a line. Our lives have two phases: one a dot, the other a line.

Our present life on Earth is the dot. It begins. It ends. It's brief. But from that dot extends a line that goes on forever. That line is eternity, which Christians will spend in Heaven.

The Dot: The Line:
Life on Earth   Life in Heaven

Right now we're living *in* the dot. But what are we living *for*? The shortsighted person lives for the dot. The person with perspective lives for the line.

This Earth (and our time here) is the dot. Our beloved Bridegroom, the coming wedding, the Great Reunion, and our eternal home in the New Heaven and New Earth—they're all on the line. That's our next key:

TREASURE PRINCIPLE KEY #4

I should live not for the dot but for the line.

The person who lives for the dot lives for treasures on Earth that rot and rust. The person who lives for the line lives for treasures in Heaven that will last forever.

Giving is living for the line.

We'll each part with our money. The only question is when. We have no choice but to part with it later. But we *do* have a choice whether to part with it now. We can keep earthly treasures for the moment, and we may derive some temporary enjoyment from them. But if we give them away, we'll enjoy eternal treasures that will never be taken from us.

This is what missionary Jim Elliot was talking about when he wrote, "He is no fool who gives what he cannot keep to gain that which he cannot lose."

If you hear those words and think, *He was one of those superspiritual types who didn't think about gain,* then you missed the point. Reread his statement. Gain was precisely what Jim Elliot was thinking about! He just wanted the gain he couldn't lose. He wanted his treasures in Heaven.

Live for the line, not for the dot.

POSSESSION OBSESSION

Some years ago, a PBS television special called *Affluenza* addressed the "modern-day plague of materialism."[15] The program revealed:

- The average American shops six hours a week while spending forty minutes playing with his or her children.

- In a given year, more Americans declare bankruptcy than graduate from college.
- In 90 percent of divorce cases, arguments about money play a prominent role.

What struck me about this program was that it didn't argue against materialism on a moral basis but a pragmatic one: Material wealth doesn't make us happy.

Listen to some of the wealthiest people of their time:

- "The care of $200 million is enough to kill anyone. There is no pleasure in it."
  —W. H. VANDERBILT
- "I have made many millions, but they have brought me no happiness."
  —JOHN D. ROCKEFELLER
- "Millionaires seldom smile."
  —ANDREW CARNEGIE
- "I am the most miserable man on Earth."
  —JOHN JACOB ASTOR
- "I was happier when doing a mechanic's job."
  —HENRY FORD

You've likely read the stories of lottery winners who are more miserable a few years after winning than they were before. The wealth they dreamed would bring them happiness didn't.

At the airport, my friend Hugh Maclellan Jr. saw an acquaintance who looked troubled.

"What's the matter?" Hugh asked.

The man sighed. "I thought I was finally going to have a weekend to myself. But now I have to go supervise repairs on my house in Florida." Dejected, he sat waiting to take off in his private jet.

We think we own our possessions, but too often they own us.

Here's a man with a lifestyle most people dream of, yet he couldn't even enjoy his weekend. He was enslaved by his possessions.

We think we own our possessions, but too often they own us.

Nothing makes a journey more difficult than a heavy backpack filled with nice but unnecessary things. Pilgrims travel light.

THE TYRANNY OF THINGS

Nanci and I have lived in our house for thirty-eight years. For the first nine years we had ugly orange carpet. We never cared what happened to it. The day we finally installed a new carpet, someone lit a candle. The match head fell off and burned a hole in the carpet.

The day before we wouldn't have cared. Now we were upset. Were we better off with our new possession?

My point, of course, isn't that carpet is bad. It's not. But every item we buy is one more thing to think about, talk about, clean, repair, rearrange, fret over, and replace when it goes bad.

Let's say I get a television for free. Now what? Maybe I subscribe to a cable or satellite service and get a streaming device. I get surround-sound speakers. I buy a recliner so I can watch my programs in comfort. This all costs money. But it also takes large amounts of time and attention.

The time I devote to my TV and its accessories means less time for communicating with my family, reading the Word, praying, opening our home, or ministering to the needy.

So what's the true cost of my "free" television?

Acquiring a possession may push me into redefining my priorities. If I buy a boat, I'll want to justify my purchase by *using* the boat, which may mean frequent weekends away from my family or church, making me unavailable to attend my grandson's football game or teach a Sunday school class.

The problem isn't the boat or the television. The problem is me. It's a law of life, the tyranny of things.

Chasing the Wind

Solomon makes a series of insightful statements in Ecclesiastes 5:10–15. Each follows with my paraphrase:

- "Whoever loves money never has money enough" (v. 10). *The more you have, the more you want.*
- "Whoever loves wealth is never satisfied with his income" (v. 10). *The more you have, the less you're satisfied.*
- "As goods increase, so do those who consume them" (v. 11). *The more you have, the more people (including the government) will come after it.*
- "And what benefit are they to the owner except to feast his eyes on them?" (v. 11). *The more you have, the more you realize it does you no good.*
- "The sleep of a laborer is sweet, whether he eats little or much, but the abundance of a rich man permits him no sleep" (v. 12). *The more you have, the more you have to worry about.*
- "I have seen a grievous evil under the sun: wealth hoarded to the harm of its owner" (v. 13). *The more you have, the more you can hurt yourself by holding on to it.*
- "Or wealth lost through some misfortune" (v. 14). *The more you have, the more you have to lose.*
- "Naked a man comes from his mother's womb, and as he comes, so he departs. He takes nothing from his labor that he can carry in his hand" (v. 15). *The more you have, the more you'll leave behind.*

As the wealthiest man on Earth, Solomon learned that affluence didn't satisfy. All it did was give him greater opportunity to chase more mirages. People tend to run out of money before mirages, so they cling to the myth that things they can't afford will satisfy them. Solomon's money never ran out. He tried everything, saying, "I denied myself nothing my eyes desired; I refused my heart no pleasure" (Ecclesiastes 2:10).

Solomon's conclusion? "When I surveyed all that my hands had done and what I had toiled to achieve, everything was meaningless, a chasing after the wind" (v. 11).

Why do we keep getting fooled? Because we imagine that the earthly treasures we see are the genuine items rather than mere shadows of true treasures.

But earthly treasures can become heavenly ones. A. W. Tozer wrote:

> As base a thing as money often is, it yet can be transmuted into everlasting treasure. It can be converted into food for the hungry and clothing for the poor; it can keep a missionary actively winning lost men to the light of the gospel and thus transmute itself into heavenly values. Any temporal possession can be turned into everlasting wealth. Whatever is given to Christ is immediately touched with immortality.[16]

If affluenza is the disease, what's the cure? If materialism is the poison, what's the antidote? Paul offers an answer in a passage I mentioned in chapter 2:

> Command those who are rich in this present world . . . to be rich in good deeds, and to be generous and willing to share. In this way they will *lay up treasure for themselves as a firm foundation for the coming age,* so that they may take hold of the life that is truly life. (1 Timothy 6:17–19)

Paul brings us right back to the Treasure Principle. The treasures we lay up in Heaven by giving are a rock-solid foundation we will build on when we get there.

I carry in my wallet a little card. On one side it says, "God owns it all. I'm His money manager." The other side says, "God cares what I do with the money He entrusts to me (I'd better ask Him)." Near this are Christ's words in Matthew 6 :19–21 and Paul's in 2 Corinthians 9:7. Keeping this near my cash and credit cards is a powerful reminder.[17]

Paul says that being "generous" and "rich in good deeds" allows us to "take hold of the life that is truly life." This is the abundant life Jesus promised, in contrast to the superficial, money-centered life that leaves us empty.

That leads to the fifth key to the Treasure Principle:

TREASURE PRINCIPLE KEY #5

Giving is the only antidote to materialism.

The act of giving is a vivid reminder that it's all about God, not about us. It's saying I'm not the point, *He* is the point. He does not exist for me. I exist for Him. God's money has a higher purpose than my affluence. Giving is a joyful surrender to a greater Person and a greater agenda. Giving dethrones me and exalts Christ. It breaks the chains of the Money-god that would enslave me.

As long as I still have something, I'm tempted to believe I own it. But when I give it away, I relinquish control. At the moment of release, the spell is broken. My mind clears. I recognize God as owner, myself as servant, and others as intended beneficiaries of what God has entrusted to me. I am free, and with freedom comes happiness.

Giving doesn't strip us of vested interests; rather, it shifts our vested interests from Earth to Heaven—from self to God.

Of course, money isn't all we can give. Time and wisdom and hands-on help are wonderful gifts. When given out of love for God and others, they too will no doubt result in treasures in Heaven. Giving in any form frees us from the gravitational hold of money and possessions. It shifts us to a new center of gravity: Heaven.

MUD PIES IN THE SLUM

When Christ returns, the world "will be destroyed by fire, and the earth and everything in it will be laid bare" (2 Peter 3:10). Does that sound depressing? It *would* be depressing if this world, as it is, were our home. But it isn't! It *would* be depressing if we couldn't use our lives and resources to make a difference for eternity. But we can!

C. S. Lewis put it this way:

> We are halfhearted creatures, fooling about with drink
> and sex and ambition when infinite joy is offered us,
> like an ignorant child who wants to go on making
> mud pies in a slum because he cannot imagine what is
> meant by the offer of a holiday at sea. We are far too
> easily pleased.[18]

Even many Christians have settled for a life of unsatisfying material acquisitions, like making mud pies in a slum.

There's something so much better than anything the world can offer—eternal treasures and exhilarating joy.

You want these treasures and this joy, don't you? But maybe you're not sure where to start. Keep reading.

6

Getting Started

*I have held many things in my hands,
and I have lost them all; but whatever I have
placed in God's hands, that I still possess.*

MARTIN LUTHER

To everyone's amazement, Sam Houston, the colorful soldier and politician, came to Christ. After his baptism, Houston said he wanted to pay half the local minister's salary. When someone asked why, he responded, "My pocketbook was baptized too."[19]

Like Sam Houston, you may understand that the Christian life is inseparable from giving. But you might be wondering, *Where do I start?*

A logical beginning place might be where God started His Old Covenant children: "A tithe of everything from the land, whether grain from the soil or fruit from the trees, belongs to the LORD; it is holy to the LORD" (Leviticus 27:30).

The meaning of the word *tithe* is "a tenth part." Ten percent was to be given back to God. There were freewill offerings too, but the 10 percent was mandatory.

Some argue that only farmers and herdsmen were expected to tithe. Were that true, it would have included a very high percentage of Israel's population. But we're told that "the people of Israel" brought in not only what they grew but also "the tithe of everything" (2 Chronicles 31:5, ESV). God doesn't speak here of just "the farmers of Israel" tithing, but "the people of Israel." If people made and sold clothing or pottery or jewelry, surely the same level of devotion to God—as evidenced by the tithe—would be expected of them too.

Proverbs 3:9 says, "Honor the LORD with your wealth, with the *firstfruits* of all your crops." God's children give to Him first, not last.

When His children weren't giving as they should, He said:

Will a man rob God? Yet you rob me. But you
ask, "How do we rob you?" In tithes and offerings.
You are under a curse—the whole nation of you—
because you are robbing me. Bring the whole tithe
into the storehouse, that there may be food in my
house. (Malachi 3:8–10)

Jesus validated the mandatory tithe, even on small things (Matthew 23:23). But there's no mention of tithing after the Gospels, except in Hebrews 7. Since it's neither commanded nor rescinded, there's some heated debate about tithing.

I believe there's a timeless truth behind giving God our firstfruits. Still, I have mixed feelings about tithing because of the ways it is misused and misrepresented. I detest legalism. I certainly don't want to impose superseded First Covenant restrictions on Christians. However, every New Testament example of giving goes beyond the tithe. None falls short of it.

After all, Jesus raised the spiritual bar for His New Covenant people; He never lowered it (Matthew 5:27–28).

TRAINING WHEELS

Maybe you believe exclusively in "grace giving" and disagree with the church fathers and others who taught that the tithe was the minimum giving requirement for Christians. But it seems fair to ask, "God, do You really expect less of me—who has Your Holy Spirit within and lives in the wealthiest society in human history—than You expected of the poorest Israelite?"

Since the majority of Christians don't believe in or practice tithing and instead embrace "grace giving," whether or not they use the term, let's consider what this actually looks like.

Studies over the past decades indicate American Christians give on average between 2 and 3 percent of their income.[20] In fact, "More than one out of four American Protestants give away no money at all—'not even a token $5 per year.'"[21]

A 2013 study found that those who *do* tithe compose "only 10 to 25 percent of the families in the church, but they often provide 50 to 80 percent of the funding."[22]

There's often a wide disparity between what churchgoers *think* they give and what they *actually* give. "A quarter of respondents in a new national study said they tithed 10 percent of their income to charity. But when their donations were checked against income figures, only 3 percent of the group gave more than 5 percent to charity."[23]

Isn't it troubling that in this wealthy society, what's inaccurately called "grace giving" amounts to only a fraction of the First Covenant standard? Whatever we're teaching about giving today is either not true to Scripture or the message isn't getting through. Or we're not being touched by God's grace, which inevitably moves hearts to give.

Tithing is God's historical method to get His people on the path of giving. In that sense, it can serve as a gateway to the joy of true grace giving. It's unhealthy to view tithing as a place to stop, but it can certainly be a good place to start.

Tithing isn't the ceiling of giving; it's the floor. It's not the finish line of giving; it's the starting blocks. Tithes can launch us into the mind-set, skills, and habits of grace giving.

Malachi 3:8 says that the Israelites robbed God by with-holding not only their mandatory tithes but also their voluntary "offerings." By giving less in their freewill offerings than He wanted them to, they were robbing God. Setting aside tithing entirely, if they could rob God with insufficient free-will offerings, can't we do the same today? Surely God hasn't stopped caring about His people's giving.

Paul encouraged voluntary giving, yet also described such giving as "obedience" (2 Corinthians 9:13). God still has expectations of us, even when our offerings are voluntary.

Of course, God doesn't expect us all to give the same amount. We're to give in proportion to how He's blessed us (Deuteronomy 16:10, 16–17).

Some say, "We'll take this gradually, starting with 5 percent." But if you believe God hasn't lowered His minimum giving standard, that's like saying, "I used to rob six convenience stores a year. This year, by His grace, I'm going to rob only three."

The point is not to rob God *less*—it's not to rob God *at all*.

True, some would be sacrificing more by giving 5 percent of their income than others would be by giving 50 or 90 percent. Certainly the affluent should never "check off the box," as if giving 10 percent automatically fulfills their obligation. The 90 percent belongs to God too. God doesn't look just at what we give. He also looks at what we keep.

I've had the privilege of interviewing many givers. In the great majority of cases they mention how tithing first stretched them to give more. They tithed and watched God provide and move their hearts deeper into His kingdom. Now, years later, some of them are giving away 50, 80, or even 95 percent of their incomes! But it was tithing that set them on the road to giving.

When I've heard such a large number of people testify to how tithing put them on the road to life-

God doesn't look just at what we give. He also looks at what we keep.

altering generosity, it's hard for me to understand the extreme animosity some have toward this practice (entire websites are devoted to opposing tithing). Yes, it has sometimes been abused, but let's not throw out the baby of tithing with the bathwater of legalism.

When God's people were robbing Him by withholding tithes and offerings, He said, "Test me in this . . . and see if I will not throw open the floodgates of heaven and pour out so much blessing that you will not have room enough for it" (Malachi 3:10).

Ironically, many people suppose they can't afford to give precisely *because* they're not giving, and therefore not experiencing God's blessing. When God's people failed to give as He called them to, He said, "You earn wages, only to put them in a purse with holes in it" (Haggai 1:6). God didn't allow their money to go far because they were stingy and disobedient.

He told them, "You hoped for rich harvests, but they were poor. And when you brought your harvest home, I blew it away. Why? Because my house lies in ruins, says the LORD of Heaven's Armies, while all of you are busy building your own fine houses" (Haggai 1:9, NLT).

How much of our harvest is blown away because we don't make giving to God a priority? If we fulfill our obligation to God first, we invite His blessing to help us pay our debts to people. But when we rob God to pay people, we rob ourselves of God's blessing. No wonder we don't have enough. It's a vicious cycle, and it takes obedient faith to break out of it.

When people tell me they can't afford to tithe, I ask them, "If your income were reduced by 10 percent would you die?" They say, "No." And I say, "Then you've admitted you can afford to tithe. It's just that you don't *want* to."

I'm not saying that it's easy to give 10 percent when you're not accustomed to it. I'm saying—and there are millions who will agree—that it's much easier to live on 90 percent or 50 percent or 10 percent of your income *inside* God's will than it is to live on 100 percent *outside* it.

Tithing is like a toddler's first steps: They aren't his last or best steps, but they're a good start. Once you learn to ride a bike, you don't need the training wheels. Once you learn to give, tithing becomes irrelevant. And if you can ride the bike without ever using training wheels, good for you.

I have no problem with people who say "we're not under the tithe," as long as they're not using that as justification for giving less than God's Old Covenant people. But the current giving statistics clearly indicate most of us need a giving jump start. If you find a gateway to generous giving that's better than the tithe, wonderful. But if not, why not start where God started His First Covenant children?

EXCELLENT GIVING

Paul said, "See that you also excel in this grace of giving" (2 Corinthians 8:7). Like piano playing, giving is a skill. With practice, we get better at it. We can learn to give more, give more often, and give more strategically by making giving something we study, discuss, and sharpen.

The Macedonian believers gave "as much as they were able, and even beyond their ability" (2 Corinthians 8:3). What does it mean to give *beyond* our ability? It means pushing our giving past the point where the figures add up. Sometimes giving will seem like it doesn't make sense, but when we do it, God provides.

Sometimes giving will seem like it doesn't make sense, but when we do it, God provides.

Years ago Scott Lewis attended a conference where Bill Bright challenged people to give one million dollars to help fulfill the Great Commission. This amount was laughable to Scott—far beyond anything he could imagine, since his machinery business was generating an income under fifty thousand dollars a year.

Bill asked, "How much did you give last year?" Scott felt good about his answer: "We gave seventeen thousand dollars, about 35 percent of our income."

Without blinking an eye, Bill responded, "Over the next year, why don't you make a goal of giving fifty thousand dollars?"

Scott thought Bill hadn't understood. That was more than he had made all year! But Scott and his wife decided to ask God to do the seemingly impossible. God came through, and with a miraculous December 31 provision, the Lewises were able to give the fifty thousand dollars. The next year they set a goal of giving one hundred thousand dollars. Again, God provided.

Sixteen years ago Scott wrote me a note saying they had passed the one-million-dollar mark in their giving. The best part is that they didn't stop.

Obviously our incomes and the amounts we give will differ, some less and some more. But we can all excel at this grace of giving!

GIVE IT NOW OR GIVE IT LATER?

People ask, "Should I give now, or should I hang on to it, hoping my investments will do well and I'll have more to give in a year?"

I respond with two questions: "How soon do you want to experience God's blessing?" and "Do you want to be sure the money goes to God's kingdom, or are you willing to risk that it won't?"

When we stand before God, I don't believe He'll say, "You blew it when you gave Me all that money before the stock market peaked."

Jesus said, "Everyone who has left houses or brothers or sisters or father or mother or children or fields for my sake will receive a hundred times as much and will inherit eternal life" (Matthew 19:29). One hundred times as much means 10,000 percent interest. That's why I don't believe it's ever wrong to give now instead of later. God can produce far greater returns on money invested in Heaven today than Wall Street or real estate ever can.

I don't believe it's ever wrong to give now.

If we don't give now we run some real risks:

- The economy may change, and we'll have less to give.

- God says we don't know what's going to happen tomorrow (James 4:13–17). Countless investors have been "absolutely sure" about getting great returns on money that disappears overnight.
- Our hearts may change, and we may not follow through with giving.
- If you procrastinate, the same heart that's prompting you to give today may later persuade you not to. As a result of postponing giving, your heart's vested interests increase on Earth and decrease in Heaven.
- Our lives may end before we've given what we intended. Zacchaeus said, "*Here and now* I give half of my possessions" (Luke 19:8). Had he waited till "there and then" he might never have been so generous.

You may think, *No problem there. I'm putting my church and ministries in my will.* By all means, do your estate planning, and give substantially to God's kingdom. But what kind of conviction does it take to part with your money once you die? You'll have no choice!

Death isn't your best opportunity to give; it's the end of your opportunity to give. God rewards acts of faith done while we're still living.

John Wesley said, "Money never stays with me. It would

burn me if it did. I throw it out of my hands as soon as possible, lest it should find its way into my heart."[24]

Wesley earned considerable book royalties—yet his goal was to give so generously as to leave virtually nothing behind when he died. He achieved his goal. While it still had value, he traded in his "Confederate" currency for treasures in Heaven.

When the Lord returns, what will happen to all the money sitting in bank accounts, retirement programs, estates, and foundations? It will burn like wood, hay, and straw, when it could have been given in exchange for gold, silver, and precious stones (1 Corinthians 3:12–13). Money that could have been used to feed the hungry and fulfill the Great Commission will go up in smoke.

The American dream is to die with as many cards in your hand as possible. But maybe we've got it backward. Maybe our strategy should be more like those card games where the winner is the one who runs out of cards first. At the end of the game, the cards left aren't an asset, but a liability.

What Will We Leave the Kids?

"What about our children?" you may ask. "Aren't we supposed to leave them all our money?" The answer is no.

Nanci and I will leave to our wonderful daughters and their families enough to be of modest help, but not enough to change their lifestyles or undercut their need to pray with and depend on their husbands. We've communicated this, and they agree with us leaving most of our estate to God's kingdom. Sure, we plan to leave personal items and something to help with our grandchildren's education. But our children won't need most of it, and we don't want to burden them with what they don't need.

It's one of our core values to be generous to our family. However, leaving a large inheritance to children is not just a missed opportunity to invest in God's kingdom. It's also rarely in the children's best interests.

Study the lives of people who've inherited significant wealth, and you'll find that, in the vast majority of cases, it's made them more unhappy and greedy. Who needs to work hard when you've got all that money? Money funds new temptations, including addictions. Leaving more to God's kingdom and less to financially independent children is not just an act of love toward God, but toward them.

In Old Testament times, leaving an inheritance was critical (Proverbs 13:22) because children couldn't afford to buy their own land and could end up enslaved. But today, inheritances are often windfalls coming to people who have more than they need. Our own children are extraordinarily wise and Christ-centered. But that's not always the case. Giving money to the unwise is pouring gasoline on a fire.

Andrew Carnegie said, "The almighty dollar bequeathed to a child is an almighty curse. No man has the right to handicap his son with such a burden as great wealth."[25] Carnegie wrote, "The thoughtful man must . . . admit to himself that it is not the welfare of children, but family pride, which inspires these enormous legacies."[26]

Today, even a middle-class estate amounts to what was once a king's ransom. When given away, what's left behind is enough to make a great difference for God's kingdom. When passed on to family, it's enough to undermine hard work, initiative, and personal responsibility.

Your adult children should love the Lord, work hard, and experience the joy of trusting God. More important than leaving your children an inheritance is leaving them a spiritual heritage. If you left your children money they didn't need, and if they were thinking correctly, wouldn't they give it to God anyway? Then why not give it to God yourself?

Let God decide how much to provide for your adult children. Once they're on their own, the money you've generated under God's provision doesn't belong to your children—it belongs to Him, and you are His appointed money manager. If *your* money manager died, what would you think if he left all *your* money to *his* children?

Why Has God Entrusted So Much to Us?

Jesus said, "Give, and it will be given to you. A good measure, pressed down, shaken together and running over, will be poured into your lap. For with the measure you use, it will be measured to you" (Luke 6:38).

The more you give, the more comes back to you, because God is the greatest giver in the universe, and He won't let you outgive Him. Go ahead and try. See what happens.

R. G. LeTourneau invented earthmoving machines. He gave away 90 percent of his income. But the money came in faster than he could give it away. LeTourneau said, "I shovel it out and God shovels it back—but God has a bigger shovel!"

God is the greatest giver in the universe, and He won't let you outgive Him.

The health and wealth gospel dishonors Christ, since any gospel that is more true in America than in Haiti is not the true gospel. Prosperity theology is built on a half-truth. God often *does* prosper givers materially. But He won't let us treat Him like a no-lose slot machine or a cosmic genie who does our bidding. Giving is a sacrifice, and sometimes we will *feel* that sacrifice. God's payoff is very real, but it comes "at the proper time," which may not be today or tomorrow but in eternity (Galatians 6:9).

God has given you considerable material blessings. Have you ever asked yourself, *Why has He provided so much?* You don't need to wonder. Paul tells us exactly why:

> Now he who supplies seed to the sower and bread for food will also supply and increase your store of seed and will enlarge the harvest of your righteousness. You will be made rich in every way so that . . .
> (2 Corinthians 9:10–11)

So that *what?* Prosperity theology would finish this sentence, "so that we might live in wealth, showing the world how much God blesses those who love Him."

But that isn't how Paul finishes it. He says, "You will be made rich in every way *so that you can be generous on every occasion*" (v. 11).

Paul is relating the sixth and final key to the Treasure Principle.

TREASURE PRINCIPLE KEY #6

God prospers me not to raise my standard of living but to raise my standard of giving.

⚷

God comes right out and tells us why He gives us more money than we need. It's not so we can find more ways to spend it. It's not so we can indulge ourselves and spoil our children. It's not so we can insulate ourselves from needing God's provision.

It's so we can give—generously.

When God provides more money, we often think, *This is a blessing.* Yes, but it would be just as scriptural to think, *This is a test.*

The money manager has legitimate needs, and the Owner is generous—He doesn't demand that His stewards live in poverty, and He doesn't resent our making reasonable expenditures.

But suppose the Owner sees us living in mansions, driving expensive cars, and paying to fly first class? Or buying only expensive clothes and electronic gadgets and eating at the best restaurants? Isn't there a point when, as His stewards, we can cross the line of reasonable expenses? Won't the Owner call us to account for squandering money that's not ours?

We don't own the store. We just work here!

We're called God's servants, and we're told it's required of us that we "prove faithful" (1 Corinthians 4:2). We're God's errand boys and girls, His delivery men and women.

We should keep that in mind when we set our salaries. We don't own the store. We just work here!

Suppose you have something important you want to get to someone who needs it. You wrap it up and hand it over to the FedEx guy. What would you think if instead of delivering the package, he took it home, opened it, and kept it?

You'd say, "The package doesn't belong to him! He's the middleman. His job is to get it from me to the person it's intended for."

Just because God puts His money in our hands doesn't mean He intends for it to stay there!

That's what Paul told the Corinthians, encouraging them to give to the needy in Jerusalem:

> At the present time your plenty will supply what they need, so that in turn their plenty will supply what you need. Then there will be equality, as it is written: "He who gathered much did not have too much, and he who gathered little did not have too little." (2 Corinthians 8:14–15)

Why does God give some of His children more than they need and others less than they need? So that He may use His children to help one another. He doesn't want us to have too little or too much (Proverbs 30:8–9). When those with too much give to those with too little, two problems are solved. When they don't, two problems are perpetuated.

God distributes wealth unevenly not because He loves some of His children more than others, but so His children can distribute it to their brothers and sisters on His behalf.

Paul said that the God who supplies seed to the sower will increase our store of seed. Why? So we can stockpile seed or eat it? No, so we can spread it out that it might bear fruit. Abundance isn't God's provision for me to live in luxury. It's His provision for me to help others live. God entrusts me with this money not to build my kingdom on Earth but to build His kingdom in Heaven.

Are you eager to plant God's money in the field of a world that needs Christ? Does the thought of giving to what will count for eternity make your heart leap? If we understood the out-of-this-world rewards, we'd join the Macedonians and beg for the privilege of giving.

GOD'S ROYALTIES

Remember that $8.2 million lawsuit against me? When the ten-year judgment period expired, our ministry board said, "Randy, you can make more than minimum wage now."

Nanci and I talked and prayed about it. At that time we decided we didn't need a higher standard of living. We didn't need a better house or car or more insurance. So, with joy in our hearts, we said, "No, thanks." (Later we discovered the abortion clinic got the judgment extended for another ten years. But we're thankful we didn't know that when we made our decision.)

The extension finally expired in 2012. A year later our ministry board significantly increased my salary. Since then I've been paid a good wage by American standards and a great wage by global standards.

We're grateful for the higher pay, and we've enjoyed being able to do a few things we weren't able to before. As the wages have increased, our personal giving has increased. Still, God was with us all those years when our salary was lower, and He always faithfully provided.

We have never been needy in the sense Paul speaks of, but we can at least identify a little with his words:

> I have learned to be content whatever the circum-
> stances. I know what it is to be in need, and I know
> what it is to have plenty. I have learned the secret of
> being content in any and every situation, whether
> well fed or hungry, whether living in plenty or in
> want. I can do everything through him who gives
> me strength. (Philippians 4:11–13)

We've continued to give away all the book royalties and have no plans to stop. We certainly don't need them, and it delights us to see God using them to touch lives all over the world.

Our circumstances have changed since I first wrote this book, but one thing hasn't changed: We still have the privilege of experiencing one of life's greatest thrills—the joy of giving.

7

For Such a Time as This

*It ought to be the business of every
day to prepare for our last day.*

MATTHEW HENRY

Alfred Nobel dropped the newspaper and put his head in his hands.

It was 1888. Nobel was a Swedish chemist who made his fortune inventing and producing dynamite. His brother Ludvig had died in France.

But Alfred's grief was compounded by dismay. He'd just read an obituary in a French newspaper—not his brother's obituary, but *his*! An editor had confused the brothers. The headline read, "The Merchant of Death Is Dead." Alfred Nobel's obituary described a man who had gotten rich by helping people kill one another.

Shaken by this appraisal of his life, Nobel resolved to use his wealth to change his legacy. When he died eight years later, he left more than nine million dollars to fund awards for people whose work benefited humanity. The awards became known as the Nobel Prizes.

Alfred Nobel had the rare opportunity to assess his life's story at its supposed end and still have the chance to change it. Before his life was over, Nobel made sure he had invested his wealth in something of lasting value.

FIVE MINUTES AFTER WE DIE

At the end of the movie *Schindler's List,* there's a heart-wrenching scene in which Oskar Schindler—who bought from the Nazis the lives of many Jews—regrets that he didn't give more of his money and possessions to save more lives. Schindler had used his opportunity far better than most. But in the end, he longed to go back and make more generous choices.

Five minutes after we die, we'll know exactly how we should have lived.

Unbelievers have no second chance to relive their lives, this time choosing Christ. But Christians also get no second chance to live life over, this time doing more to invest in God's kingdom. We have one brief opportunity—our lifetime on Earth—to use our resources to make a difference.

John Wesley said, "I judge all things only by the price they shall gain in eternity." Missionary C. T. Studd wrote, "Only one life, 'twill soon be past; only what's done for Christ will last."

Five minutes after we die, we'll know exactly how we

should have lived. But God has given us His Word so that we don't have to wait to die to find out. And He's given us His Spirit to empower us to live that way now.

Ask yourself, *Five minutes after I die, what will I wish I would have given away while I still had the chance?* When you come up with an answer, why not give it away now? Why not spend the rest of your life closing the gap between what you'll wish you would have given and what you really are giving?

Nobel managed to change his legacy in this world. You have the far more strategic opportunity to change your legacy in the world to come.

When you leave this world, will you be known as one who accumulated treasures on Earth that you couldn't keep? Or will you be recognized as one who invested treasures in Heaven that you couldn't lose?

Put yourself in Alfred Nobel's shoes. Find a piece of paper and a pen. Sit down; think about it; then write your own obituary. Make a list of what you'll be remembered for. Go ahead.

Done? Now read your obituary. How do you feel about it?

Try writing it again, this time from the perspective of Heaven. Do you think God is pleased with your earthly life?

Maybe you're living a life that's Christ centered, with few regrets. Maybe you're daily laying up treasures in Heaven.

Or maybe not. You may be discouraged by what you've written. If so, don't lose hope. The good news is that you're still here! Like Alfred Nobel, you have the opportunity—with God's empowerment—to edit your life, and thereby your legacy, into what you want it to be.

THE GIFT OF GIVING

In Romans 12, Paul lists seven spiritual gifts, including prophecy, serving, teaching, mercy, and giving. I'm convinced that of all these gifts, giving is the one least thought about in the Western church.

Of course, all of us are called to serve, show mercy, and give, even if we don't have those specific gifts. But I believe that in different times of history God has sovereignly distributed certain gifts more widely (such as the gift of mercy during devastating plagues).

Suppose God wanted to fulfill His plan of world evangelization and help an unprecedented number of suffering people. What gift would you expect Him to distribute widely? Why not the gift of giving? And what might you expect Him to provide for those to whom He's given that gift? Perhaps unprecedented wealth to meet those needs and further His kingdom.

Look around. Isn't that exactly what God has done? The

question is, what are we doing with the wealth He's entrusted to us?

We regularly see the gift of teaching and know what it looks like. We know of prayer warriors and Bible students, but rarely do we know of people giving large percentages of their incomes to the Lord.

It's increasingly common for Christians in accountability groups to ask one another the tough questions: "Have you been spending time in the Word?" "Are you living in sexual purity?" or "Have you been sharing your faith?" But how often do we ask, "Are you winning the battle against materialism?" or "How are you doing with your giving?"

When it comes to giving, churches operate under a "don't ask, don't tell" policy. We lack communication, accountability, and modeling. It's as if we have an unspoken agreement: I won't talk about it if you won't, so we can continue living as we are.

When it comes to giving, churches operate under a "don't ask, don't tell" policy.

Think about it. If a young person wants to learn how to teach, pray, or lead a group, the church provides many examples to learn from. But how does a young Christian learn to give? Where can he or she go to see what giving looks like in the life of a believer captivated by Christ? Why are we surprised when, seeing no alternative examples, our young people take their cues from a materialistic society?

We're to "consider how we may spur one another on toward love and good deeds" (Hebrews 10:24). Shouldn't we then be asking how we can spur one another on toward giving?

Some may object, "But we shouldn't compare each other's giving." Yet Paul tells the Corinthians about the Macedonians' giving, saying he's making a comparison to motivate them (2 Corinthians 8:7–8).

Dixie Fraley Keller told me about some friends of hers. She said, "They're such an example of the art of giving. Every year we try to outgive each other!" Isn't that spurring one another on? Don't we need to help one another raise the bar of giving so we can learn to jump higher?

Scripture tells us not to give *in order to* be seen by men (Matthew 6:1). Certainly we should be careful to avoid pride. But Jesus also said in the same sermon, "Let your light shine before men, that they may see your good deeds and praise your Father in heaven" (Matthew 5:16). Through an unfortunate misinterpretation of biblical teaching, we've hidden giving and therefore hidden its joy and deprived God of glory. We've failed to draw Christians toward giving. And they lack gladness and purpose because of it.

Years ago, when our missions pastor returned from Sudan, he told our church about enslaved Christians in that region. Spontaneously, several families decided to forgo giving Christmas presents that year and instead give toward freeing slaves. The fourth-grade class at our school raised thousands of dollars for this purpose through work projects. One sixth-grade girl took the fifty dollars she'd saved up to play on a basketball team and gave it to help Sudanese believers.

One family had saved hundreds of dollars to go to Disneyland. Their child asked if they could give the money to help the slaves instead. Before long, people had given sixty thousand dollars to redeem slaves. We never even took an offering, but the giving was contagious. People told one another their giving stories. When they did, it encouraged the body to give more. It was one of the church's finest hours, and the key was hearing how God moved people to give.

King David told the people exactly how much he'd given to build the temple. The precise amounts of gold and precious stones given by the leaders were also made public. "The people rejoiced at the willing response of their leaders, for they had given freely and wholeheartedly to the LORD" (1 Chronicles 29:6–9). The people could rejoice and follow their leaders' example only because they knew how generous those leaders had been. Unless we learn how to humbly tell one another our giving stories, our churches will not learn to give.

It would have been an incalculable loss to my spiritual

life not to hear the stories of Hudson Taylor, George Müller, Amy Carmichael, and R. G. LeTourneau. Knowing what God did in and through them has been an inspiration to ask Him to do more in and through me.

A SENSE OF DESTINY

The fact that you're reading these words is likely part of God's plan to change your life—and in turn to change history and eternity.

Remember what Mordecai said to Esther? "For if you keep silent at this time, relief and deliverance will rise for the Jews from another place, but you and your father's house will perish. And who knows whether you have not come to the kingdom for such a time as this?" (Esther 4:14, ESV).

Just as Esther was in a position of privilege, so is nearly everyone reading this book. Are you educated and literate? Do you have food, clothing, shelter, a car, and one or more digital devices? Then you are among the privileged, the world's wealthy.

It's no accident that you live in this time and place in history.

Why has God sovereignly entrusted you with wealth? For such a time as this. When I think about the resources Nanci and I have and the giving opportunities the Lord blesses us with, I can't help but feel that we're part of something much larger than our little corner of the world.

Giving to God's great causes infuses us with a sense of destiny. It's no accident that you live in this time and place in history.

Scripture tells us, "For we are God's workmanship, created in Christ Jesus to do good works, which God prepared in advance for us to do" (Ephesians 2:10). Let's ask God, "What are the good works You have prepared me to do in my lifetime, starting today?" Surely most of those good works will involve being generous with our time, gifts, and money.

Is God calling you to be a more generous giver? Is He calling you to share with others the liberating joy of the Treasure Principle?

You've heard of prayer warriors. What about giving warriors? God has entrusted us with so much. Perhaps He is raising up a great army of givers and calling us to enlist. If Warren Buffet can reach out to billionaires and successfully challenge them to give away most of their wealth, shouldn't greater things happen in the church of Jesus? Shouldn't people at every income level encourage one another to experience the joy of giving?

How can you lead the way in the journey of generosity? Why not set a figure you can live on, then tell God that everything He provides beyond that amount you'll give back to

Him? When you do that, the desire to make more money takes on a kingdom purpose. It's transformed into a desire to help others more and expand God's kingdom!

We have no way of knowing how long our prosperity will last. Why not give away the abundance while we still can? Let's give until our hearts are more in touch with God's kingdom work than with our remodeling projects, business ventures, dream vacations, or retirement plans. Let's ask God if He wants us to hold off from building our dream house here, realizing that our Bridegroom's already building our dream house in Heaven. Meanwhile, we can use God's funds to build something that won't go up in smoke but will last for eternity.

THOUGHTS TO CONSIDER

"How much is God leading me to give above and beyond, in freewill offerings?" Only God can answer that question. That means we need to ask Him. He hasn't established one set amount or percentage for voluntary offerings. Maybe that's precisely so we will pray and seek His guidance, which He promises (James 1:5). It's our job to listen and obey.

Does obeying God in giving or anything else sound burdensome? On the contrary: "This is love for God: to obey his commands. And his commands are not burden-some" (1 John 5:3). Those who obey God find such joy in it that they say, "How I delight in your commands!" (Psalm 119:47, NLT).

Giving should start with your local Bible-believing, Christ-centered church, the spiritual community to which you're accountable (Galatians 6:6; 1 Corinthians 9:9–12). Beyond that, you can generously support worthy missions and parachurch ministries, carefully evaluating them by biblical standards.[27]

People ask me, "Should I support secular organizations?" It's fair to ask whether the Humane Society, as good as it may be, is as close to God's heart as evangelism, church planting, or helping the poor in Christ's name. Many people support so-called Christian colleges that no longer believe their doctrinal statements and now lead students astray. With all the godly ministries and schools we could support, why give God's money to institutions that oppose His agenda? For almost every good secular organization, there's a Christian organization doing the same work—but with an eternal perspective. When there's a choice, why not support organizations characterized by biblical standards and the supernatural work of God's Spirit?

Why not ask God how you might share the Treasure Principle (the concept or the book) with others? Perhaps you'll be like the people who led D. L. Moody and Billy Graham to Christ—you may influence others to give far more than you ever can.

Consider setting up a Bible study or discussion group, perhaps using this book. You and the group might enjoy the companion Treasure Principle video series available on DVD or via streaming from RightNow Media.[28] Or you could use the Crown Financial Ministries material on money or giving.[29] Ask God to point out those within your unique sphere of influence that you can talk with, study with, or pray with, those you can mentor or be mentored by. (Remember, I make no profit from this book; I mention these resources because I sincerely want you to benefit from them.)

MY GIVING COVENANT

Here's a six-step plan to help you apply the Treasure Principle, a giving covenant between you and God. I encourage you to read it, discuss it with your spouse or friends, and pray about it.

If you sense God leading you to make a new commitment to giving, I encourage you to sign the abbreviated version of the covenant at the end of this book.

1. I affirm God's full ownership of me (1 Corinthians 6:19–20) and everything entrusted to me (Psalm 24:1). I recognize that "my" money and possessions are His. I'm His money manager and His delivery person. I will ask Him what He wants me to do with His money.

2. I will set aside the firstfruits—starting with at least 10 percent—of all I receive, treating it as belonging exclusively to the Lord. I do this in obedience to Him, desiring His blessing (Malachi 3:6–12). By faith I take God up on His challenge to test Him in this.

3. Out of the remaining treasures God entrusts to me, I will seek to make generous freewill gifts. I recognize that God has entrusted wealth to me so that I can be "generous on every occasion" (2 Corinthians 9:11). Realizing I can rob God by withholding not only the tithe but also whatever offerings He calls on me to give (Malachi 3:8), I ask Him to make His will clear to me.

4. I ask God to teach me to give sacrificially to His purposes, including helping the poor and reaching the lost. I commit myself to avoiding indebtedness so that I don't tie up His funds and therefore have greater freedom to follow the Spirit's promptings to give.

5. Recognizing that I cannot take earthly treasures from this world, I determine to store them up as heavenly treasures—for Christ's glory and the eternal good of others and myself. Affirming that Heaven, not Earth, is my home and Christ is my Lord, I commit myself to lay out His assets before

Him regularly—leaving nothing as untouchable—and ask His direction for what to do with and where to give His money. I'll start with this question: "What am I hanging on to that You want me to give away?"

6. Recognizing that God has given me my family, my friends, my church, and others in my circle of influence, I ask Him to help me share the Treasure Principle so they, too, may experience present joy and future rewards.

THE GREATEST PLEASURE

There's only one statement of Jesus recorded in Acts that doesn't appear in the Gospels. Perhaps God did that so it would stand out:

> The Lord Jesus himself said: "There is more happiness in giving than receiving." (Acts 20:35, GNT)

Let's not be so absorbed with "getting what's ours" that we miss what brings real happiness: giving God what's His. Giving is doing what we were made for: loving God and our neighbors (Matthew 22:36–40). Giving boldly and joyfully affirms Christ's lordship.

A vivid example of this joy is found in Charles Dickens's classic story *A Christmas Carol*. When the story begins, Ebenezer Scrooge is wealthy, horrendously greedy, and miserable. After encounters with three spirits on Christmas Day (the day on which God's Greatest Gift was born), he is given a second chance. I'm struck by the description of the transformed Scrooge:

Giving is doing what we were made for: loving God and our neighbors.

> He went to church, and walked about the streets,
> and watched the people hurrying to and fro, and
> patted children on the head, and questioned beggars,
> and looked down into the kitchens of houses, and up
> to the windows; and found that everything could
> yield him pleasure. He had never dreamed that any
> walk—that anything—could give him so much
> happiness.[30]

After his transformation, Scrooge, giddy with delight, walks through the streets, freely distributing his wealth to the needy. He, who only yesterday scoffed at the idea of charity, now takes his greatest pleasure in giving. Ebenezer Scrooge, who had been miserable and inflicted his misery on others, now becomes profoundly and contagiously happy.

On the story's final page, Dickens says of Scrooge:

Some people laughed to see the alteration in him,
but he let them laugh, and little heeded them. . . .
His own heart laughed, and that was quite enough
for him. And it was always said of him, that he
knew how to keep Christmas well, if any man alive
possessed the knowledge.[31]

What was the source of Scrooge's happy transformation? Gaining an eternal perspective. Through supernatural intervention, Scrooge was allowed to see his past, present, and still-changeable future through the eyes of eternity. Let's ask God for the same insight.

Ebenezer Scrooge leaped for joy because he'd discovered the antidote to the materialism that had poisoned his soul. Scrooge learned exactly what this book is about: the secret of joyful giving.

Do you want to experience this kind of joy? I invite you to transfer your assets from Earth to Heaven. I encourage you to give humbly, generously, and frequently to God's work. Excel in giving so that you may please God, serve others, find new meaning and pleasure in your present life, and enjoy treasures one day in Heaven.

I urge you to embrace Christ's invitation: "Give, and it will be given to you" (Luke 6:38). Then when He gives you more, remind yourself why: that you may be more generous than ever before.

I invite you to send your treasures on to Heaven, where they will safely await you. When you do, you'll embrace the freedom, experience the joy, and sense the smile of God.

When you give, you'll feel His pleasure.

Treasure Principle

You can't take it with you—
but you *can* send it on ahead.

TREASURE PRINCIPLE KEYS

GOD OWNS EVERYTHING. I'M HIS MONEY MANAGER.
*We are the managers of the assets
God has entrusted—not given—to us.*

MY HEART ALWAYS GOES WHERE I PUT GOD'S MONEY.
*Watch what happens when you reallocate your
money from temporal things to eternal things.*

**HEAVEN AND THE FUTURE NEW EARTH,
NOT THIS FALLEN ONE, IS MY HOME.**
*We are citizens of "a better country—a heavenly one"
(Hebrews 11:16).*

I SHOULD LIVE NOT FOR THE DOT BUT FOR THE LINE.
*From the dot—our present life on Earth—extends a
line that goes on forever, which is eternity in Heaven.*

GIVING IS THE ONLY ANTIDOTE TO MATERIALISM.
*Giving is a joyful surrender to a greater person and a
greater agenda. It dethrones me and exalts Him.*

**GOD PROSPERS ME NOT TO RAISE MY STANDARD
OF LIVING BUT TO RAISE MY STANDARD OF GIVING.**
*God gives us more money than we need so
we can give—generously.*

MY GIVING COVENANT

1. I affirm God's full ownership of me and everything entrusted to me.

2. I set aside the firstfruits—at least 10 percent—of every wage and gift I receive as belonging exclusively to the Lord.

3. Out of the remaining treasures God entrusts to me, I seek to make generous freewill gifts.

4. I ask God to teach me to give sacrificially to His purposes, including helping the poor and reaching the lost.

5. Recognizing I cannot take earthly treasures from this world, I determine to lay them up as heavenly treasures—for Christ's glory and the eternal good of others and myself.

6. I ask God to show me how to lead others to the present joy and future reward of the Treasure Principle.

Signed: _____

Witness: _____

Date: _____

31 Radical, Liberating Questions to Ask God About Your Giving

Asking specific questions of God is a great tradition in Scripture.

At a pivotal point in his life (2 Samuel 2:1–2), David asked the Lord two very specific questions:

> *"Shall I go up to one of the towns of Judah?"* he asked.
> The LORD said, "Go up."
> David asked, *"Where shall I go?"*
> "To Hebron," the LORD answered.

As God's children, we should ask and seek and knock (see Matthew 7:7). His answers won't always be as direct as they were to David, but He invites us to ask Him nonetheless.

When it comes to financial stewardship, how God leads you will be different in many details than how He leads me. He hasn't handed each of us a standardized checklist with boxes to mark off. Rather, He has provided us His Word with stewardship principles we must wrestle with. In the process of this struggle, God expects us to seek His face and to pursue counsel from godly believers.

Financial stewardship decisions require wisdom beyond our own. Scripture says, "If any of you lacks wisdom, he should ask God, who gives generously to all without finding fault" (James 1:5).

Do you truly desire God's wisdom and empowerment in making difficult stewardship decisions (and evaluating your own heart)? *Then ask.* He won't leave you in the dark. He has given you His Word and His Spirit to guide you.

The following thirty-one questions are designed to assist you. After each question, I've listed a key passage of Scripture as well as other passages I'd encourage you to look up. (You can ponder consecutively as many as you wish or meditate on one per day for a month.) God promises that His Word won't return to Him without accomplishing the purpose for which He sent it (see Isaiah 55:11). So in each of these brief meditations, focus first and foremost on the scriptures and secondarily on the questions.

Ask the Holy Spirit to speak to your heart and give you direction. He will. Count on it.

QUESTIONS TO ASK GOD

1. Lord, in Your Word, You make a direct connection between experiencing grace and expressing grace through giving. So does the degree of my giving suggest that I have recognized and embraced Your grace?

> See that you also excel in this grace of giving. . . .
> For you know the grace of our Lord Jesus Christ,
> that though he was rich, yet for your sakes he
> became poor, so that you through his poverty
> might become rich. (2 Corinthians 8:7, 9)
>
> See also 2 Corinthians 9:15 and Romans 8:32.

2. Father, have You raised me up for such a time as this? Is it more than a coincidence that You have entrusted me with many financial resources in a time when the poor and unreached have such pressing needs and there are unprecedented opportunities to help them?

> And who knows whether you have not come
> to the kingdom for such a time as this? (Esther
> 4:14, esv)
>
> See also Acts 17:26 and Ephesians 2:10.

3. Father, what am I guarding and keeping for myself that's preventing me from depending wholeheartedly on You? Which of "my" assets can I give to You, so that You, not money and things, will be my center of gravity?

> No servant can serve two masters. Either he will
> hate the one and love the other, or he will be

devoted to the one and despise the other. You
cannot serve both God and Money. (Luke 16:13)

See also Psalm 42:1–2 and Matthew 5:6.

4. Lord, am I honoring You as owner of the assets You've
   entrusted to my care? Or am I treating You as a mere
   financial consultant, to whom I pay a fee (2 percent,
   10 percent, or . . .)? Have I been acting as if I own the
   store and You work for me rather than recognizing that
   You own it and I work for You?

   The land is mine and you are but aliens and my
   tenants. (Leviticus 25:23)

   See also Deuteronomy 10:14 and 1 Chronicles
   29:11–12.

5. Where in my community do You want me to partici-
   pate in meeting physical and spiritual needs through
   Christ-centered ministries? The inner city? Prison
   ministry? Pro-life work? Is a short-term missions trip
   or long-term service overseas part of Your exciting plan
   for me and my family?

   [Josiah] defended the cause of the poor and
   needy, and so all went well. Is that not what it
   means to know me? (Jeremiah 22:16)

See also Proverbs 28:27 and Romans 10:13–15.

6. Lord, why have You entrusted me with greater financial blessings than I once had? Is it to raise my standard of giving? Do I really see myself as Your delivery person, or do I assume You put things in my hands so I can keep them?

> You will be made rich in every way so that you can be generous on every occasion, and through us your generosity will result in thanksgiving to God. (2 Corinthians 9:11)

> See also 2 Corinthians 8:14 and Acts 11:29.

7. Lord Jesus, have I overaccumulated? Have I allowed unwise spending and accumulating debt to inhibit my giving to You? Have I said, "There's not enough left to give," while maintaining spending habits that make *sure* there's not enough to give?

> Honor the LORD with your wealth, with the firstfruits of all your crops; then your barns will be filled to overflowing, and your vats will brim over with new wine. (Proverbs 3:9–10)

> See also Proverbs 22:7 and 1 Corinthians 16:2.

8. Lord, I've sometimes wondered why You're not blessing me more financially. Could it be that I've been spending money on myself first rather than giving You the firstfruits? Have I placed myself under Your discipline?

> "Is it a time for you yourselves to be living in your paneled houses, while this house remains a ruin?"
>
> Now this is what the LORD Almighty says: "Give careful thought to your ways. You have planted much, but have harvested little. You eat, but never have enough. You drink, but never have your fill. You put on clothes, but are not warm. You earn wages, only to put them in a purse with holes in it. . . .
>
> "You expected much, but see, it turned out to be little. What you brought home, I blew away. Why?" declares the LORD Almighty. "Because of my house, which remains a ruin, while each of you is busy with his own house. Therefore, because of you the heavens have withheld their dew and the earth its crops." (Haggai 1:4–6, 9–10)

See also Malachi 3:8–11 and Luke 6:38.

9. Lord, have I fallen for the lie that I don't have enough to give, despite the fact that the greatest examples of giving in Scripture were poor people?

> Calling his disciples to him, Jesus said, "I tell you the truth, this poor widow has put more into the treasury than all the others. They all gave out of their wealth; but she, out of her poverty, put in everything—all she had to live on." (Mark 12:43–44)

> See also 2 Corinthians 8:1–4 and Galatians 6:9–10.

10. Father, would it honor You if I determined a basic level of income sufficient to live on, then simply gave away whatever You provide beyond that? In the process, would You teach me to be more grateful and content?

> He who loves money will not be satisfied with money, nor he who loves wealth with his income. (Ecclesiastes 5:10, ESV)

> See also Hosea 13:6 and Philippians 4:11–13.

11. Lord Jesus, since financial assets will burn at Your Second Coming, will the assets I've stored up on Earth be wasted if You return in my lifetime?

> But the day of the Lord will come like a thief.
> The heavens will disappear with a roar; the
> elements will be destroyed by fire, and the
> earth and everything in it will be laid bare.
>
> Since everything will be destroyed in this
> way, what kind of people ought you to be?
> (2 Peter 3:10–11)
>
> See also Ecclesiastes 5:15 and 1 Corinthians
> 9:24–25.

12. Lord, does the fact that You entrusted Your money to
    me indicate You want *me*—during my lifetime—to
    invest it in eternity rather than passing along that
    responsibility to my children? Once my children have
    finished college or are working on their own, would
    inheriting my wealth (beyond reasonable gifts and
    items of sentimental or heritage value) be a complicat-
    ing or even corrupting influence?

    > An inheritance quickly gained at the beginning
    > will not be blessed in the end. (Proverbs 20:21)
    >
    > See also Proverbs 13:11; 17:26 and 1 Corinthi-
    > ans 4:2.

13. How can I be sure that the assets You've entrusted to
    me will serve You after I die? I want to be generous to

my children and grandchildren but don't want to make them independent of You. If they are adults not needing my financial support, should I give away now what I can and, when I die, leave more of what remains to my church and missions or ministries that are close to Your heart?

> Come, you who are blessed by my Father; take your inheritance, the kingdom prepared for you since the creation of the world. For I was hungry and you gave me something to eat. (Matthew 25:34–35)

> See also 1 Peter 1:3–4 and Colossians 3:23–24.

14. Father, what's the eternal downside in giving as much as I can give to You now? In contrast, what's the eternal downside of minimizing or delaying my giving?

> Whoever can be trusted with very little can also be trusted with much, and whoever is dishonest with very little will also be dishonest with much. So if you have not been trustworthy in handling worldly wealth, who will trust you with true riches? And if you have not been trustworthy with someone else's property, who will give you property of your own? (Luke 16:10–12)

See also Luke 19:17; Mark 10:29–30; and
2 Corinthians 5:9–11.

15. Lord, if I delay giving now, is it possible the money may
disappear or I may die before I get a chance to give it?

> Show me, O LORD, my life's end and the
> number of my days; let me know how fleeting
> is my life.
>
> You have made my days a mere hand-
> breadth; the span of my years is as nothing
> before you. Each man's life is but a breath.
>
> Man is a mere phantom as he goes to and
> fro: He bustles about, but only in vain; he heaps
> up wealth, not knowing who will get it. (Psalm
> 39:4–6)

See also Ecclesiastes 5:13–14; 8:8.

16. If I don't release my resources now for Your kingdom
causes, will I be in danger of becoming more wrapped
up in earthly, rather than heavenly, treasure?

> Command those who are rich in this present
> world not to be arrogant nor to put their hope in
> wealth, which is so uncertain, but to put their
> hope in God, who richly provides us with

everything for our enjoyment. Command them to do good, to be rich in good deeds, and to be generous and willing to share. (1 Timothy 6:17–18)

See also Matthew 6:21 and Hebrews 3:15.

17. Lord, will I rob myself of joy and reward and rob You of my trust by holding on to significant assets I could have joyfully given to You?

Not that I am looking for a gift, but I am looking for what may be credited to your account. (Philippians 4:17)

See also Hebrews 9:27 and Ephesians 6:8.

18. Father, Wall Street can't touch the eternal returns of investing in Your kingdom. So why are my eyes so often focused on temporary, earthly investments with such pitifully small returns? Lord, please broaden my perspective, increase my faith, and expand my eternal-investment mentality.

Everyone who has left houses or brothers or sisters or father or mother or children or fields for my sake will receive a hundred times as much and will inherit eternal life. (Matthew 19:29)

See also Hebrews 6:10 and 2 Corinthians 4:18.

19. Lord, please help me to see clearly *where* best to give Your money. How can I determine which recipients will most benefit from the money I give and which will likely mismanage it? Help me be not only a generous giver but a wise one.

> And this is my prayer: that your love may abound more and more in knowledge and depth of insight, so that you may be able to discern what is best. (Philippians 1:9–10)

> See also 1 Timothy 5:3–5 and Proverbs 14:7.

20. You commended Zacchaeus for giving away half of all he had, seeing it came from a transformed heart. We are Jesus followers, just like those people two thousand years ago. You've never changed Your opinions about giving generously, have You? God, would You empower me to trust You enough to act in obedience to You for the good of the needy?

> But Zacchaeus stood up and said to the Lord, "Look, Lord! Here and now I give half of my possessions to the poor, and if I have cheated anybody out of anything, I will pay back four times the amount."

Jesus said to him, "Today salvation has come to this house, because this man, too, is a son of Abraham." (Luke 19:8–9)

See also Matthew 19:21 and Luke 14:33.

21. If I were to make a list of all the assets You've entrusted to me, Lord, and ask what You want me to give away, is there *anything*—house, car, real estate, retirement funds, bank accounts—that I'm treating as untouchable?

The earth is the LORD's, and everything in it, the world, and all who live in it. (Psalm 24:1)

See also 1 Corinthians 6:19, Psalm 50:12, and Haggai 2:8.

22. Father, without realizing it, am I making money my God-substitute? Am I failing to experience the pleasures that can be found only in You?

My soul thirsts for You, my flesh yearns for You, in a dry and weary land where there is no water. (Psalm 63:1, NASB)

See also Colossians 3:4–6 and Psalm 34:8.

23. When I meet You face to face, will I wish I had given away more? God, help me by Your grace to close the

gap between what I'm giving now and what I'll one day wish I had given.

> Watch out! Be on your guard against all kinds of greed; a man's life does not consist in the abundance of his possessions. (Luke 12:15)

> See also 2 Corinthians 8:7 and Acts 10:1–4.

24. Lord, I know you call me to be wise, but am I focused on saving to the point of hoarding and stockpiling like the rich fool instead of trusting You?

> Therefore do not worry about tomorrow, for tomorrow will worry about itself. Each day has enough trouble of its own. (Matthew 6:34)

> See also Proverbs 3:5–6 and Philippians 4:6, 19.

25. Father, are material assets competing with You for lordship over my life? Have I been giving enough to experience a joyful liberty from the tyranny of money and things?

> For we brought nothing into the world, and we cannot take anything out of the world. But if we have food and clothing, with these we will be content. But those who desire to be rich fall into temptation, into a snare, into many

> senseless and harmful desires that plunge
> people into ruin and destruction. For the love
> of money is a root of all kinds of evils. It is
> through this craving that some have wandered
> away from the faith and pierced themselves
> with many pangs.
>
> But as for you, O man of God, flee these
> things. Pursue righteousness. (1 Timothy
> 6:7–11, ESV)

See also Ezekiel 28:4–5 and Revelation 3:17–18.

26. What specifically am I hanging on to that You want
    me to give away? Since You promise me, "It is more
    blessed [happy-making] to give than to receive," what
    happiness awaits me by letting go and becoming more
    of a giver?

    > A generous man will himself be blessed, for
    > he shares his food with the poor. (Proverbs
    > 22:9)

    See also Acts 20:35 and 2 Corinthians 8:13–15.

27. Jesus, how can I better communicate with and pray
    with my spouse and children so we can walk together
    down this exhilarating road of giving?

So commit yourselves wholeheartedly to these
words of mine. Tie them to your hands and
wear them on your forehead as reminders. Teach
them to your children. Talk about them when
you are at home and when you are on the road,
when you are going to bed and when you are
getting up. (Deuteronomy 11:18–19, NLT)

See also 2 Corinthians 9:7 and Ephesians
5:22, 25.

28. What am I doing—and what *should* I be doing—to
train the children in my sphere of influence to be
regular, joyful, and generous givers?

Train a child in the way he should go, and
when he is old he will not turn from it.
(Proverbs 22:6)

See also 1 Corinthians 11:1; 16:2.

29. Lord, I realize that in most places around the world, I
would be regarded as extremely wealthy (even if I am
lower or middle class in this place and time). Have You
put so much into my hands because You have blessed
me with the gift of giving? What have I been missing
out on by not exercising this gift to a greater degree?

> In Christ we who are many form one body, and
> each member belongs to all the others. We have
> different gifts, according to the grace given us.
> If a man's gift is prophesying, let him use it in
> proportion to his faith. If it is serving, let him
> serve; if it is teaching, let him teach; if it is
> encouraging, let him encourage; if it is contrib-
> uting to the needs of others, let him give
> generously. (Romans 12:5–8)

> See also 2 Corinthians 9:7 and Galatians 6:9.

30. If I am a giver, whom have I been teaching and
    mentoring in giving? In a spirit of humility, how can I
    share with others the joy of giving?

> For I know your eagerness to help, and I have
> been boasting about it to the Macedonians, telling
> them that since last year you in Achaia were ready
> to give; and your enthusiasm has stirred most of
> them to action. (2 Corinthians 9:2–3)

> See also 1 Chronicles 29:1–14 and Hebrews
> 10:24.

31. Father, please empower me to live each day here as I
    will wish I'd lived five minutes after I die. Help me

look forward to Heaven and the New Earth and to storing up treasures there. I long to hear from You say, "Well done, good and faithful servant. . . . Enter into the joy of your lord" (Matthew 25:21, NKJV). What steps can I take to help make this happen?

> For the Son of Man is going to come in his Father's glory with his angels, and then he will reward each person according to what he has done. (Matthew 16:27)

> See also Proverbs 19:17 and Matthew 10:42.

Questions and Answers
About the Treasure Principle

As part of this updated edition, I've already addressed directly or indirectly some of the good questions I've received. Here are several more I'd like to answer:

Does living by the Treasure Principle mean only buying what's essential and forgoing vacations or dinners out? Is this "poverty theology"?

In a public discussion with other Christian leaders, a well-known evangelical pastor and speaker claimed that John Piper, David Platt, Francis Chan, and I promote "poverty theology." He said I've developed a theology based on my legal situation, which required me to "have nothing." The implication is that I encourage other people to "have nothing."

I often encourage people to go to globalrichlist.com and insert their household income to see where they figure in terms of global wealth. Most will find they land in the top 1 or 2 percent.

If you look at what I possess, it's safe to say I am still among the wealthiest people in the world. Nanci and I own a comfortable, though nonextravagant house and have access to two decent used cars. Even when our income was limited, we never "had nothing." We ate out sometimes then and went on vacations, as we do now.

In the middle of a passage where Paul says the rich should be commanded to be generous and willing to share, he also says that God gives us "everything for our enjoyment" (1 Timothy 6:17). Poverty is never our goal, and God is happy for us to do some things with our money (His money entrusted to us) that help us enjoy life.

What I challenge in my books and in my teaching is the materialistic assumption that when God entrusts us with wealth, we should just spend it on ourselves, without considering God's kingdom and other people's needs.

I wrestle with my degree of wealth relative to most of the world, and it appears to me that Platt, Chan, and Piper (all of whom I know and respect) do the same. In this materialistic culture, all of us should ask, "How much is too much (to spend or keep)?" We do this not to embrace guilt or poverty but to follow Jesus as our Lord and to extend love to others.

I encourage all believers: let's give generously for God's glory, people's good, and our gladness. I would describe that not as a "poverty theology," but simply a biblical, Christ-centered theology of grace, gratitude, and generosity.

When pastors preach on giving or pass out The Treasure
Principle *to their congregations, isn't that self-serving,
since they stand to gain from people giving to their
churches?*
Naturally, like all of us, pastors need to examine their motives in all they do (1 Peter 5:2). Some pastors do talk too
much about money and seem to focus on making the local
church a storehouse of wealth rather than a clearinghouse
that sends funds out into the community and the world.

Nevertheless, I believe that pastors should preach "the
whole counsel of God" (Acts 20:27, ESV).

Scripture includes so much about money and giving that
it's ethically impossible to ignore it. Pastors should teach
these passages despite their fears that people might question
their motives. (Pastors have told me this is why they avoid
preaching on giving.) They should also lead the way in giving generously and modeling wise stewardship.

While obeying God is sufficient reason to instruct people about giving, notice what Philippians 4:17 says. Paul explains his invitation for the church to give: "Not that I am
looking for a gift, but I am looking for what may be credited
to your account."

He's giving people an opportunity to support his ministry not because he needs their gift (if they don't give, he
knows God will provide through other means). Rather, he's

doing this *for their sake,* that God may credit it to their account in Heaven.

Calling on them to obey God's call to generous giving is acting in their best interests. Why? Because their giving of temporary earthly treasures will result in eternal treasures in Heaven. What pastor would want his people to fail to receive eternal rewards because he failed to teach them what God says about giving? Encouraging people to give generously is doing them a great favor!

Finally, since giving is inseparable from God's grace, and God's grace is what we need more than anything, surely we want to cultivate and encourage God's grace in our churches.

———

Do you believe the Old Covenant model of tithing still applies to Christians today?

While I dealt with tithing in chapter 6, I'll say more in response to this common question.

Some teach that anyone who sees value in the practice of tithing is guilty of legalism. Certainly some are, but I think tithing still has merit for getting people started in the adventure of giving.

I believe in the New Covenant's superiority over the Old (Romans 7; 2 Corinthians 3; Hebrews 8). However, the models of giving God the firstfruits (with tithing as the minimum) and giving freewill offerings beyond that have ongoing value.

The question is not whether tithing is the whole of Christian giving. It certainly isn't!

Christ fulfilled the entire Law, but He didn't render it irrelevant. When it comes to the Old Testament, we must be careful not to disregard ongoing principles intended for everyone simply because they're in the same books as detailed regulations intended only for ancient Israel.

Some argue against tithing by saying, "The New Testament advocates voluntary offerings." Yes, but so does the Old Testament, which is filled with freewill giving. Having a minimum standard of giving has never been incompatible with giving above and beyond it.

Ten percent is not some lofty goal; it's just a starting place. But getting started is important. If starting at 10 percent seems legalistic, then I suggest starting at 11 or 12 percent. But beginning with less than 10 percent is setting the bar low. Since the Law required 10 percent as a minimum (counting just the tithe to the priests and Levites) from people in a poor culture, surely the transforming work of the Holy Spirit could be expected to produce significantly more in our affluent culture.

The disciples freely gave to meet the needs of others, even liquidating major assets to do so, because "much grace was upon them all" (Acts 4:33). It was obvious from the beginning that being under grace didn't mean that New Testament Christians would give less than their Old Testament brethren. Hearts transformed by the grace of Jesus trust God more, love others more, and therefore give more.

———

I'm financially strapped and have nothing to give. So what am I supposed to do except feel guilty?

You can find creative ways to free up funds in your budget to give to God's kingdom. I realize it isn't easy, especially if you've already attempted to cut superfluous spending. But honestly, sometimes we simply don't want to forego expenditures that would allow us to give more but cost us something we want.

I've been in countries where people who make less than one hundred US dollars a year wouldn't dream of giving less than 10 percent—and often give considerably more. Since we live in the most affluent society in history—where what we call "poverty level" is considerably above the average standard of living of most societies in all of history—it's odd to suppose we couldn't give 10 percent.

Pray and ask God to provide. If He is big enough to create and redeem you, isn't He big enough to take care of you when you step out in faith? Following God's commands to be generous may require trust, but you'll find the payoff—which includes joy and gratitude—is great.

———

Shouldn't I get out of debt first before I start tithing, or at least before I ever give beyond a tithe?

If we take God's Word seriously, we should avoid debt when we can, since "the borrower is servant to the lender" (Proverbs 22:7).

In rare cases where we do accumulate debt, for instance to buy a reasonably priced house, we should only borrow an amount small enough to allow us to make affordable payments and seek to pay off the debt early if we can. We may need to say no to some or many of our wants, but we shouldn't say no to obedience or generosity.

If God commands and encourages us to give and lay up treasures in Heaven, and He certainly does, let's not wait until we're out of debt to obey Him. Debt reduction is important, but not as important as giving to God's kingdom.

You will ultimately be in a better place to give by reducing your debt, but it's also true that when we give, God is pleased and will honor our efforts to pay off our debts. So give generously to the Lord—not instead of striving to eliminate your debt but in concert with it.

———

You wrote that Malachi 3 speaks of robbing God "by withholding tithes and offerings." How could people be robbing God by withholding a freewill offering? That seems like a contradiction.

At first glance, this objection appears to make sense. But Malachi 3:8 clearly says his people were robbing God by withholding tithes *and* voluntary offerings. I think this passage, by including not just tithes but offerings, demonstrates God has a will for our lives that goes beyond the minimal directives of Scripture. Read it for yourself and see whether you agree.

There's no law saying I must share Christ with the person sitting next to me on a plane, but often I believe God wants me to do so. It's freewill evangelism for me, but God can still prompt me to do it. When He does, I think I should obey Him.

We've been created to do good works, "which God prepared in advance for us to do" (Ephesians 2:10). The wording indicates God has a particular will as to what good works we should do. This suggests He has in mind specific amounts and recipients of our giving, which we should ask Him about.

God calls us to freewill Bible study, prayer, and church attendance. But that doesn't mean He has no specific will for us in those areas. God calls us to freewill offerings, but He can certainly desire that we be more generous in our giving. God may be saying, "I won't tell you the exact amount to give, because you need to ask Me personally, listen to My promptings, and then do it, for My joy and for yours."

———

I'm troubled by the parable of the man who finds the treasure in a field, hides it, then without telling the owner, buys the field so he can possess the treasure. Surely Jesus wouldn't teach us to do something unethical.
First, this treasure in the story should likely be assumed to have been buried long ago, perhaps by a stranger on the run, and not by the current landowner. It was long forgotten. Obviously, had the landowner buried it, he'd simply dig it up before selling his land.

Second, parables were a form of communication that stressed one central idea. The rest of the story is somewhat extraneous, serving mainly to help convey the primary meaning.

In hermeneutics class, one of my professors warned us, "Never make a parable walk on all fours." In other words, don't try to make it say more than it really intends to say, which always relates to its primary point, not its supporting details. Christ's lesson is about the enduring value and joy of discovering great treasure that represents His eternal kingdom, which is worth everything we might give up to obtain it.

Isn't it cruel to tell impoverished Christians in developing countries that they should give? Doesn't that impossible expectation lay guilt on them?

Giving is a timeless principle and privilege that God invites all His people to enjoy. It brings both rewards and dignity. Amounts given vary widely, but the principle of Gospel generosity is constant among God's people.

What God teaches about money and possessions wasn't written for wealthy Christians in North America but for all people in all times in all places. Believers in poor countries are often the greatest examples of generosity.

Second Corinthians 8–9, the longest and perhaps most significant passage on giving in Scripture, starts with focusing on the Macedonians who lived in "extreme poverty" and gave "beyond their ability" and with "overflowing joy." They "urgently pleaded with us for the privilege" of giving. We shouldn't deprive the poor of this privilege.

Is it cruel to preach on giving to those who don't have much? I believe it's cruel *not* to preach on giving, because it's part of the whole counsel of God. If we withhold the Bible's teaching on generosity, we act as God's editors rather than His messengers. (Remember, it's rich people, not poor people, who are the exceptions in Scripture and in history!)

God says, "Test me in this" and watch Me provide (see Malachi 3:10). By not telling people about giving, we rob them of the joy of trusting God and seeing His provision.

I've spoken on Matthew 6 in Kenya and Cuba, but I changed the illustrations so they corresponded to the means and opportunities available to the intended audiences. Likewise, I've encouraged those translating *The Treasure Principle* in other parts of the world to make my illustrations more culturally appropriate. But God has called all His children in all times and places to give.

———

How can we possibly do anything to "earn" eternal rewards?

Let's be sure this is perfectly clear: Salvation and rewards are very different. Salvation is something we cannot possibly earn and to which we can contribute absolutely nothing (Ephesians 2:8–9; Titus 3:5).

Our redemption doesn't involve our works. It is purely Christ's work. However, our works *do* affect our reward. Just as there are eternal consequences to our faith, so there are eternal consequences to our works.

Because we speak of rewards so rarely, it's easy to confuse God's work and man's. We may, for example, mistakenly believe that Heaven is a person's reward for doing good things.

False! Eternal life is entirely "the free gift of God" (Romans 6:23, ESV). Entrance to Heaven is a gift, not a reward.

In regard to salvation, our work for God is no substitute for God's work for us. In regard to rewards, God's work for us is no substitute for our work for God. Of course, ultimately, even our reward-earning works are empowered by the Holy Spirit (Colossians 1:29).

We can't earn our salvation—nothing could be clearer. Yet can you read 1 Corinthians 9:24–27, about running hard to win the crown, without the sense that by God's grace Paul is striving to earn eternal rewards? Isn't that his point?

Still, because some people will inevitably confuse rewards with salvation, which cannot be earned, I prefer not to say we earn rewards but instead that God graciously chooses to give them to us. Regardless, God promises to reward us specifically for our obedience. In regard to the Treasure Principle, as we saw in chapter 2, at least five passages specifically link the rewards of treasures in Heaven with our choices to give to the needy in this life (Matthew 6; Matthew 19; Mark 10; Luke 12; and 1 Timothy 6).

Let's call on God to empower us to obey Him, in giving and in every other aspect of our lives. And let's look forward to the day when He might say to us, "Well done, my good and faithful servant."

———

*Doesn't talking about treasures in Heaven encourage
legalistic living rather than a desire to do good works
out of love for Christ?*

Paul said, "I count everything as loss because of the surpass-
ing worth of knowing Christ Jesus my Lord" (Philippians
3:8, ESV). Since gaining Christ makes everything else seem
comparatively worthless, shouldn't Christ alone be the treasure we seek? Doesn't focusing on rewards make us self-
conscious, not Christ-conscious?

The answer is that the same apostle Paul who said everything is worthless compared to knowing Jesus, also said we
should labor for rewards:

> Do you not know that in a race all the runners run,
> but only one gets the prize? Run in such a way as to
> get the prize. . . . They do it to get a crown that will
> not last; but we do it to get a crown that will last
> forever. (1 Corinthians 9:24–25)

Paul assures Christians, "God 'will give to each person
according to what he has done'" (Romans 2:6). He writes,
"You know that the Lord will reward everyone for whatever
good he does" (Ephesians 6:8). The apostle says, "I have fin-
ished the race, I have kept the faith. Now there is in store for
me the crown of righteousness, which the Lord, the righ-
teous Judge, will award to me on that day—and not only to

me, but also to all who have longed for his appearing" (2 Timothy 4:7–8).

Paul delights in the reward he will receive in fellowship with the Thessalonian Christians, in whom he invested his life: "For what is our hope, our joy, or the crown in which we will glory in the presence of our Lord Jesus when he comes? Is it not you?" (1 Thessalonians 2:19). And, as we've seen, Paul declared that we should give generously in order to lay up treasures for ourselves in the world to come (1 Timothy 6:18–19).

Whatever Paul was saying in Philippians 3 can't be contradictory to what he said in these other passages.

Christ, our greatest Treasure, is also our great rewarder. He said, "For the Son of Man is going to come in his Father's glory with his angels, and then he will reward each person according to what he has *done*" (Matthew 16:27). To say Christ is the main treasure we seek is absolutely true. To say He is the only treasure is false, since He himself told us to store up treasures in Heaven.

When I get pushback on this, I point out that I didn't say "store up for yourselves treasures in Heaven"! If you don't like it, your argument is with the One who first said it: Jesus.

Pitting rewards against Christ imagines a conflict that simply doesn't exist. God tells us we "must believe . . . that he rewards those who earnestly seek him" (Hebrews 11:6). To believe God is a rewarder is to believe exactly what He tells us.

It's misguided to regard any motive besides love for God as unacceptable. In His Word, God gives us a variety of motives—including love for people, fear of disobedience, and hope of reward. These should not be seen as *mixed,* impure motives, but rather as *multiple* God-given motives. Don't we need as many motives as possible to do the right thing?

We dare not discount rewards out of fear of legalism any more than we should disregard Bible study, fasting, and prayer because we fear being legalistic about them. Sure, legalism can always enter the picture, but godly, grace-motivated people should embrace God's promise of reward, never rejecting it as unspiritual. Let's leave it to God to decide what's spiritual and what isn't.

———

What stories have people told you about experiencing the joy of giving through practicing the Treasure Principle?

I've seen people give hundreds of acres of land to Christian ministries, downsize their homes, sell their businesses, and give away the money to help the needy. I've seen them travel around the world in the cause of global missions. One person, who read some of these same principles in one of my novels, moved overseas years ago to serve underground churches in China. She wrote me, "I've never known such joy."

A successful businessman told me that after reading *The Treasure Principle* he now knows why God blessed him financially. It's not so he can drive nicer cars and live in a bigger house. It's to build God's kingdom.

I told him about several missions groups and pro-life projects and ways to help persecuted Christians. I wish you could have heard his excitement as he determined to liquidate more earthly assets and dramatically expand his eternal investment portfolio! Guilt had nothing to do with it. It was all about privilege and sheer happiness.

This man followed through, and over the years he's given more and more. His happiness is real, and it's contagious! May the same be true of us all.

In a far better world, in the presence of Jesus, God's children will gather for feasts. We will meet face-to-face and eat and drink and laugh and exchange stories with those whose giving to us changed our lives and with those whose lives God changed through our giving. Those treasures await us in Heaven.

What could be better?

Key 1:
God owns everything.
I'm His money manager.

We are the managers of the assets God has entrusted—not given—to us.

Key 2:
My heart always goes
where I put God's money.

*Watch what happens when you reallocate your money
from temporal things to eternal things.*

_____

_____

_____

_____

_____

_____

_____

_____

_____

_____

_____

_____

Key 3:
Heaven and the future New Earth, not this fallen one, is my home.

We are citizens of "a better country—a heavenly one"
(Hebrews 11:16).

_____
_____
_____
_____
_____
_____
_____
_____
_____
_____
_____
_____
_____
_____

——— ❧ ———

Key 4:
I should live not for
the dot but for the line.

*From the dot—our present life on Earth—extends a line
that goes on forever, which is eternity in Heaven.*

Key 5:
Giving is the only
antidote to materialism.

*Giving is a joyful surrender to a greater person and
a greater agenda. It dethrones me and exalts Him.*

Key 6:
God prospers me
not to raise my standard
of living but to raise
my standard of giving.

*God gives us more money than we need
so we can give—generously.*

_____
_____
_____
_____
_____
_____
_____
_____
_____
_____

———— ❦ ————

Reflections on
31 Questions to Ask God

_____

_____

_____

_____

_____

_____

_____

_____

_____

_____

_____

_____

_____

_____

_____

_____

_____

—— ❧ ——

Notes

1. Randy Alcorn, *Money, Possessions, and Eternity,* rev. ed. (Carol Stream, IL: Tyndale House, 2003).
2. John Piper, *Desiring God, Twenty-Fifth Anniversary Reference Edition* (Colorado Springs, CO: Multnomah, 2011), 287.
3. Logos Bible Software, Bible Sense Lexicon, www.logos .com.
4. Bible Sense Lexicon.
5. J. P. Louw and E. A. Nida, eds., *Greek-English Lexicon of the New Testament: Based on Semantic Domains,* vol. 1 (New York: United Bible Societies, 1996), 620.
6. Craig L. Blomberg, *Matthew: An Exegetical and Theological Exposition of Holy Scripture,* The New American Commentary (Nashville, TN: Holman Reference, 1992), 123.
7. Stephen King, "What You Pass On," *Family Circle,* November 1, 2001, 156.
8. T. Boone Pickens, quoted in Mary Toothman, *Ledger,* "Speaking at FSC, T. Boone Pickens Says He Was 'Put Here to Make Money' So He Could Give It Away," September 22, 2014, www.theledger.com/news/2014

0922/speaking-at-fsc-t-boone-pickens-says-he-was
-put-here-to-make-money-so-he-could-give-it-away.

9. Bill Gates, "A Strategy Is Essential When Giving to
   Charity," *Deseret News,* March 28, 1999, www.
   deseretnews.com/article/688151/A-strategy-is-essential
   -when-giving-to-charity.html?pg=all.

10. Beth Duff-Brown, "Bill Gates Donates $100 Million
    to India AIDS Fight," Associated Press, *Seattle Post-
    Intelligencer,* November 2002, www.seattlepi.com
    /news/article/Gates-AIDS-donation-to-India-aimed
    -at-protecting-1100698.php.

11. "Angelina Jolie's Double Life," *Reader's Digest,* Novem-
    ber 2004.

12. Stephen M. Silverman, "Angelina: U.N. Work a Gift,
    After My Kids," *People,* October 12, 2005.

13. See Randy Alcorn, *In Light of Eternity: Perspectives on
    Heaven* (Colorado Springs, CO: WaterBrook, 1999).

14. John Bunyan, quoted in Bruce Wilkinson, *Walk Thru
    Eternal Rewards* workbook, Walk Thru the Bible
    Ministries.

15. John de Graff, *Affluenza,* September 15, 1997, PBS
    documentary.

16. A. W. Tozer, *Born After Midnight* (Harrisburg, PA:
    Christian Publications, 1959), 107.

17. See http://store.epm.org/product/wallet-giving-cards.

18. C. S. Lewis, *The Weight of Glory, and Other Addresses* (New York: Macmillan, 1949), 3–4.

19. Sue Flanagan, *Sam Houston's Texas* (Austin, TX: University of Texas Press, 1964), 121.

20. "How Evangelicals Give," *Christianity Today,* January 31, 2011, www.christianitytoday.com/ct/2011/february /howevangelicalsgive.html.

21. Christian Smith, Michael O. Emerson, and Patricia Snell, *Passing the Plate: Why American Christians Don't Give Away More Money* (Oxford University Press, 2008), quoted in Rob Moll, "Scrooge Lives!," *Christianity Today,* December 5, 2008, www .christianitytoday.com/ct/2008/december/10.24.html.

22. Church Law and Tax Group, "State of the Plate," quoted in Melissa Steffan, "An Inside Look at Church Attenders Who Tithe the Most," *Christianity Today,* May 17, 2013, www.christianitytoday.com/gleanings /2013/may/inside-look-at-church-attenders-who-tithe -most.html.

23. David Briggs, "The Flesh Is Weak," *Huffington Post,* September 1, 2012, www.huffingtonpost.com/david -briggs/the-flesh-is-weak-churchgoers-give-far-less-than -they-think_b_1846516.html.

24. John Wesley, *Letters of John Wesley* (New York: Hodder and Stoughton, 1915), 66.

25. Andrew Carnegie, quoted in Lee Jenkins, *Taking Care of Business: Establishing a Financial Legacy for Your Family* (Chicago: Moody Publishers, 2001), 230.

26. Andrew Carnegie, *The Autobiography of Andrew Carnegie and His Essay The Gospel of Wealth* (Mineola, NY: Dover, 2014), 282.

27. For help in evaluating organizations, see Randy Alcorn, "Nineteen Questions to Ask Before You Give to Any Ministry," Eternal Perspective Ministries, www.epm.org/19questions.

28. For details see www.rightnow.org/Content/Series/198062#Trailer.

29. For a selection of these Bible studies, contact Crown Financial Ministries at www.crown.org, or see "The Treasure Principle" series video online at www.rightnow.org/Content/Series/325.

30. Charles Dickens, *A Christmas Carol* (Philadelphia: John C. Winston, 1939), 128.

31. Dickens, *A Christmas Carol*, 131.

Resources to Help You with Giving and Money Management

Generous Giving
www.generousgiving.org
407-650-3663; 423-755-2399

Ronald Blue & Company
www.ronblue.com
800-841-0362

Crown Financial Ministries
www.crown.org
800-722-1976

Eternal Perspective Ministries
www.epm.org
Includes articles, audios, and videos by Randy Alcorn
503-668-5200

National Christian Foundation
www.ncfgiving.com
800-681-6223

The Gathering
www.thegathering.com
903-509-9911

Kingdom Advisors
www.kingdomadvisors.com
404-497-7680

Generosity Path
www.generositypath.org

Stewardship Partners
www.stewardshippartners.com
800-930-6949

Excellence in Giving
www.excellenceingiving.com
719-329-1515

I Like Giving
www.ilikegiving.com
info@ilikegiving.com

About the Author

Randy Alcorn is the founder and director of Eternal Perspective Ministries (EPM). Prior to 1990, when he started EPM, he served as a pastor for fourteen years. He has spoken around the world and has taught on the adjunct faculties of Multnomah University and Western Seminary in Portland, Oregon.

Randy is the best-selling author of over fifty books with more than ten million sold. His books have been translated into more than seventy languages. Randy has written for many magazines and produces the popular periodical *Eternal Perspectives*. He's been a guest on over eight hundred radio and television programs, including *Focus on the Family, The Bible Answer Man, Family Life Today, Revive Our Hearts, Truths That Transform,* and *Faith Under Fire.*

The father of two married daughters, Karina Franklin and Angela Stump, Randy lives in Gresham, Oregon, with his wife and best friend, Nanci, and their golden retriever, Maggie. They are the proud grandparents of five grandsons: Jake, Matt, Ty, Jack, and David. Randy enjoys hanging out with his family, biking, underwater photography, research, and reading.

You may contact Eternal Perspective Ministries by e-mail through their website at www.epm.org or at 39085 Pioneer Blvd., Suite 206, Sandy, OR 97055 (503) 668-5200.

**Visit Randy Alcorn's blog at
www.epm.org/blog.**

**Connect with Randy also at
www.facebook.com/randyalcorn
and www.twitter.com/randyalcorn.**

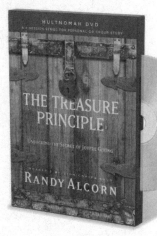